The Big Book of Welding for Beginners

An Instruction Handbook to Weld, Cut, and Shape Metal with 10 Welding Projects Included Plus Tips, Tricks and Tools to Get You Started

By

Luke Wade

Copyright © 2021 – Luke Wade

All rights reserved

No part of this publication may be reproduced, distributed, or transmitted in any form or by any means, including photocopying, recording, or other electronic or mechanical methods, without the prior written permission of the publisher, except in the case of brief quotations embodied in reviews and certain other non-commercial uses permitted by copyright law.

Disclaimer

This publication is designed to provide competent and reliable information regarding the subject matter covered. However, the views expressed in this publication are those of the author alone, and should not be taken as expert instruction or professional advice. The reader is responsible for his or her own actions.

The author hereby disclaims any responsibility or liability whatsoever that is incurred from the use or application of the contents of this publication by the purchaser or reader. The purchaser or reader is hereby responsible for his or her own actions.

Table of Contents

Introduction 7

Chapter 1 9

Essentials of Welding 9

    What is Welding? 9

    History of Welding 11

    Profiting From Welding 15

Chapter 2 21

Basic Welding Terminologies 21

Chapter 3 32

Welding Tips and Tricks 32

Chapter 4 39

Getting Started With Welding 39

    Tools and Supplies 39

        Metal 39
        Welders 45
        Welding Wire 53

Shielding Gas 55
Welding Table 56
Welding Clamps 57
C Clamp 58
Oxy-Acetylene Setup 59
Angle Grinder 60
Wire Brush 60
Sheet Welding Gauge 60
Speed Square 61
Chop Saw 61
Tape Measure 62
Slag Hammer 62
Welding Torch 62
MIG Pliers 63
Soapstone 63
Metal File 64
Helmet 65
Safety Glasses 65
Gloves 66
Welding Magnets 66
Welding Framing Jig 67
Setting Up Your Welding Workshop 67

Welding Hazards and Safety Precautions 72

Welding Positions and Joints 76

Cleaning and Preparing Metal 84

Undoing Welds 86

Finishing Your Welds 90

Chapter 5 96

Welding Techniques 96

MIG – Gas Metal Arc Welding (GMAW) 96

TIG – Gas Tungsten Arc Welding (GTAW) 103

Stick – Shielded Metal Arc Welding (SMAW) 109

Flux Corded Arc Welding (FCAW) 111

Oxyacetylene Welding 113

Chapter 6 118

Welding Projects Ideas 118

Classic Horseshoe Puzzle 118

Welded Steel Planters 121

Floating Chain Wine Bottle Holder 124

Steel Prototype Fabrication 126

Garden Vines Metal Trellis 131

Mini Atomium 134

Steel Rose 138

Bar Stool 141

Steel and Coffee Sack Footstool 145

Metal Base Outdoor Table 149

Chapter 7 153

Resolving Common Welding Mistakes 153

Chapter 8 167

Welding Frequently Asked Questions 167

Introduction

Now, you have decided to learn welding, let me give you a mental preparation to help you in your learning journey; it is very easy to get overwhelmed by the amount of information you have to consume. Almost every professional welder scaled through this bridge of gaining knowledge and is still in the business of gaining knowledge. Beginning your welding journey without the right measure of knowledge on the basic things could frustrate you in the long run. You need a solid and well-grounded understanding of the concept of welding, what it entails, the ways through which you can make money in welding, the techniques and processes involved in welding, common terminologies used to describe simple processes, sample projects, and steps required in making them, common mistakes in welding and how to avoid them, tools used in welding, amongst many other things. This knowledge needs to be established in your heart before you start your welding journey.

I can't imagine you starting welding without a well-balanced knowledge of these things. How would you know the welding technique that is best to use and how to go about it? It could be disastrous; ignorance could be very costly. Some of these things are easy to learn, many others are difficult.

Some welding procedures produce clean beads that are visually attractive and require little or no adjustment or correction. Some procedures produce something exactly the opposite. How would you discover the means to get the particular result that you desire? What type of metals will allow you to make a specific design? What type of metal should you use in making certain welding projects?

All these questions and many others would be answered in this book, so read with an inquisitive and curious mindset.

Let's jump right in.

Chapter 1

Essentials of Welding

What is Welding?

Welding is a systematic process of fabricating materials like metals or thermoplastics by using high heat in melting the parts together and allowing them to fuse when they cool down. This process ensures the joining of materials and is very different from brazing and soldering, which are lower temperature metal joining techniques that do not melt the base metal.

Welding involves a much higher temperature joining technique. It not only melts the base metal, it also adds a chemical material to the joint to form a thick pool of molten material (the weld pool). This weld pool is also addressed as filler material.

This additional filler can only be achieved if the heat is very high and up to the welding level. This is why brazing and soldering don't provide the same weld pool. The heat that is generated in the process of this metal-joining cannot join together a solid metal that firmly; it cannot create the weld pool, which acts as a firm joiner.

Irrespective of the weld configuration, when two iron gets joined together, the filler is sometimes thicker, and the weld pool after it has cooled off will be very firm, even much more than the base material.

In some cases, the heat can be pressured during the welding process to produce a strong weld. It is the duty of the welder to garner protection for the metal filler and secure it from contamination and oxidation.

Also, note that there are different energy sources for welding, operating with different intensities of heat.

The energy source in use and project type determines the flow of the welding process. However, in general, welding is an industrial activity of processing and joining metals that can be carried in any comfortable environment, e.g., open-air, inside a workshop, under water and outer space.

Metal joining can be hazardous, especially when higher heat than usual is involved, as in the case of welding. During operation, it is very important to remain guarded or shielded to avoid vision damage, electric shock, and other work hazards.

Welding has actually been around for many years; forge welding is the only welding process that has been available for several years. It gained popularity in the 19th century. This welding has been existing for a very long time and was used by blacksmith millennials to join base iron metals together. The process involves the heating and hammering of base materials in fiery furnaces and intense heat.

Today welding has gone much more advanced and is way simpler and easier with less complicated tools.

As developments began to come up, they were many technical inventions; the latest invention in welding today is robot welding. It is the most popular welding type. The robot welding technique has been developed time after time, even as science seems to advance. Up to date, scientists are still working to invent better methods of welding.

History of Welding

The history of welding metals can be traced many years back to several millennia. It is not erroneous to state that the joining of metals is as old as man. However, the oldest record in history comes from the Bronze and Iron Ages in Europe and the Middle East. These times were very spectacular in the development of welding.

Herodotus, a Greek historian, recorded in the 5th Century book that Glaucus of Chios was the first man who invented iron welding single-handedly. Then many other persons began to adapt to the process also. In India around 310 AD, an iron pillar of 5. 4 metric tons was constructed in Delhi, India through welding. To date, it is called the pillar of Delhi.

The bronze and Iron age quickly passed and introduced us to the Middle Age. The middle-age introduced a high measure of advancement in the invention of forge welding. The blacksmiths forged metal by pounding it and heating it repeatedly until bonding occurred. Some scientists began to make documented research on welding as a process. One of the scientists, Vannoccio Biringuccio, published a paper in 1540 named De la pirotechnia, which includes a detailed description of the forge welding operation. In a short time, renaissance craftsmen became well educated and advanced in the craft of forging; the practice became common amongst many in the industry.

Another scientist named Sir Humphry Davy invented the short-pulse electrical arc in 1800 and made public his discoveries in 1801. This discovery was worked upon by a Russian scientist Vasily Petrov in 1802. His invention was named the continuous electric arc. His work became popular in a short time, even more popular than the first invention by Sir Humphry. In this paper, he described the process he went through in making the experiments; he also talked about the stable arc discharge and how it is used in making applications. One unique usage he mentioned was the truth that the forge can be used in melting metals.

Not too long after, in the early 17th century, Davy, another scientist who wasn't aware of Petrov's work, came up with his own discovery of the continuous electric arc. In 1881-82, Russian scientist Nikolai Benardos and Polish scientist Stanisław Olszewski developed the first electric arc welding method. This welding method can also be called carbon arc welding. It involves the use of carbon electrodes. More arc welding inventions were made and metal electrodes by several scientists from different places.

A. P. Strohmenger made a unique invention, something different from the usual in 1900. He developed a coated metal electrode in Britain, which produced an unusually stable arc. A Russian scientist named Vladimir Mitkevich in 1905 proposed making a three-phase electric welding arc. This wasn't adopted at the time, and then another inventor came up with alternating current welding in 1919.

Inventions continued for a very long time, even till the beginning of the 20th century. It seems there was always something more to uncover and some deeper phase of welding. Resistance welding was also developed and patented in 1885 by Elihu Thomson. He went further to make advances for more than 15 years after. In 1893, Thermite welding and oxyfuel welding was invented and duly established in 1893. Acetylene welding was discovered in 1895, but it came into use in 1900.

For a very long time, oxyfuel welding was the most accepted welding method because of its simplicity, portability and affordability. However, it didn't thrive after the 20th century, it was sidelined due to its limitations in industrial applications. Many more advances in metal coverings were made over time, and many people replaced oxyfuel welding with arc welding.

Some other developments continued to spring up eventually, including the invention of electron beam welding in 1958. Complex machines were created that enabled you to make technical welds through the focused heat source. Laser beam was debuted in 1960, after the introduction of the laser. It provides excellent speed and an automated welding process, which is way easier. Other industrial welding type like the Magnetic pulse welding (MPW) was invented in 1967. Wayne Thomas made another invention called the Friction stir welding in 1991. It was launched at The Welding Institute in the UK. It was easily accepted into the market because it has more high-quality applications than other welding types worldwide. These four new inventions are quite pricey as a result of the high cost of equipment required. This expensiveness is its major limitation.

Profiting From Welding

Any craft can be monetized; however, there is a need to be educated on the hows in monetizing a craft. There is no stereotyped way to monetize all the craft; for some individual crafts like welding, there are unique tips on how to make money from welding.

Welding is not just any craft; it is a professional technique that can easily be mastered if followed appropriately. Also, if you get to know the ropes in welding, money could pour into your hands from it. Asides from that, you can use the knowledge for personal benefits. For instance, you can repair your metallic tools that got spoilt.

Of course, it is not a profession, and welding is not a business you can just start with any degree, let's say a degree in business management. It is more of a physical skill than an intellectual knowledge that should be possessed. You would have to start from the simple processes, techniques, models, and the only way you can master the things you need to learn before welding as a business; this process is practice and education.

Irrespective of you being a professional or beginner, you can make money from home with foundational knowledge.

When you start welding from home, you won't have many people patronizing you, but don't let that discourage you. You can go to the market to get a price for your products before you start selling them. While doing this, get a brand name and try to build on it. Once you have established the brand name, you will get a higher range of patronage because you have built trust and professionalism over time.

Here is a list of projects that you can make at home;

- Metal Furniture

This is one thing that sells well in the market. People love to change their furniture from time to time, even if it isn't made according to their specifications. People just love to have good and attractive furniture in their homes. You should ensure that you deliver aesthetic and unique designs while maintaining the highest order quality. If your metal furniture is really made with quality, you will build a decent sales opportunity through customer recommendations. You can weld metal chairs, tables and racks as a beginner. Refrain from trying complex innovations when you can start on a basic level.

You can start building in bulk and giving discounts as an incentive to encourage new customers.

- Car Ramps

The target market for this product is garages, car enthusiasts and businessmen. They will be more interested than anyone would. Focus your marketing energy on them and spread the word to market your brand. Unlike furniture, the car ramps are usually customized. Don't try to make them in bulk, you can only receive specifications from your customers before you build and you can also make a sample to show around during your project marketing.

Endeavor to adhere to the specifications and deadlines when given, this is the way to attract clients and keep them.

- Metal Interior Decorations

This is a booming hit, as everyone would love to beautify their house in a way it looks relaxing and comfortable. Metal decorations are a perfect replacement for many customized materials that used to be pretty expensive. The metal alternative is not expensive in itself. They don't require any form of extensive or maintenance cost.

Feel free to innovate your ideas; people won't want to pay for a copied idea; a creative and original work will win you a place in people's hearts.

- BBQ Grills

This project is quite simple, and not much goes into it at once. Hence, the cost of production is quite low. Yet you can trade it for a really huge amount, many persons do not know how to weld this and if you have got meat lovers around you, that's a plus. You can focus all your energy on this field and try to perfect it; you would be making more money than anyone in t. Things like this, when people hear that you are specialists in a particular field, help them trust the process.

In doing things like this, ensure that your quality is guaranteed and unique.

- Yard Art

Animal posing as a type of yard art refers to making creative structures like animal models. You can focus on this niche also because it involves creative art. You also focus on making models. You can also make animal skeletons and other aesthetic designs.

Chapter 2

Basic Welding Terminologies

Several common terminologies are used in welding. They help you to understand and appreciate the process of welding fully.

In this chapter, we will be looking at the basic welding terms.

Acceptable Weld – This is a weld that happens to meet the applicable requirements.

Braze Welding – A welding process using a flame that can liquify the filler metal beneath the base metals' solid-state and above 842 F.

Actual Throat – This term is used to describe the shortest distance between the face of a fillet weld and its root.

Gas Welding – This is a technical welding process where a gas flame is used in creating welding heat. It is much highly effective than other welding processes.

Air Carbon Arc Cutting – Air carbon arc cutting process involves removing a molten metal with a jet of air by variation.

Backhand Welding – When this technique is used in welding, the gun flame is fully directed to the finished weld.

Base Metal – a term used to refer to a metal that has undergone the process of welding, brazing, soldering, or cutting.

Bevel – This is a shape of metal that has an angular edge. It is formed in the middle of the cut surface and a theoretical plane perpendicular to the plate surface.

Carbon-Arc Welding – In this welding method, an arc is used to create fusion between a carbon electrode and the metal to be welded.

Air Hardening – This term refers to the process whereby steel is made hardened by the coolness of the air that it is exposed to. This doesn't need to be necessarily applicable when the object to be hardened has a good level of thickness. Another name that is used to describe this term a fully hardened metal.

Pressure Welding – A welding process of using pressure to make a weld.

Metal-Arc Welding – A welding process where an arc is used in producing the heat to form a weld by fusing metal materials and electrodes to weld the metals together.

Alternating – This term refers to a process where an electrical current travels alternately in several directions in a current conductor.

Bond – A point or process of joining or welding metal and base metal.

Anneal – This is a welding process that involves heating a base metal to a very low-temperature level. This process is immediately followed by an averagely progressive cooling rate to increase softness in the metal and eliminate stresses.

Arc Length – The distance between the workpiece's point of attachment and the electrode.

Arc Time – The time taken in maintaining an arc when making an arc weld.

Arc Voltage – during welding, there is a voltage that cuts across the arc of the welder.

Brittleness – The possibility of a base metal to break due to failure.

Buildup – A variation on the work surface in which extra material is on the metal to receive the expected dimensions.

Carbide Precipitation – When a metal is heated for too long or cooled slowly after a total transformation, atoms and elements of carbon move to the grain boundaries. When the atoms combine with themselves, they become carbides. This seeming attraction between carbon and chromium forms a thin inter-granular layer of chromium carbides.

Casehardening – This is a heat-treatment process that is given to steel alloys, in the outer part is harder than the interior. The level of hardness depends on the length of treatment.

Cast steel – This term is used to describe a solidified molten steel in a weld mold.

Cold Working – This is a permanent distortion or disorganization of metal by heating it below a very low crystallization temperature. This results in hardening.

Complete Fusion – Here is fusion on the top of the total faces; it is the fusion between all close weld beads.

Composite Electrode – An electrode that mechanically consists of one metal and more compound component of metal used in arc welding.

Conductor – Material containing a good number of loosely bounded electrons and can move freely and easily when electrical pressure is applied. All metals are potential conductors.

Constricted Arc – This refers to a plasma arc put in shape by tightening the orifice in the plasma arc torch nozzle.

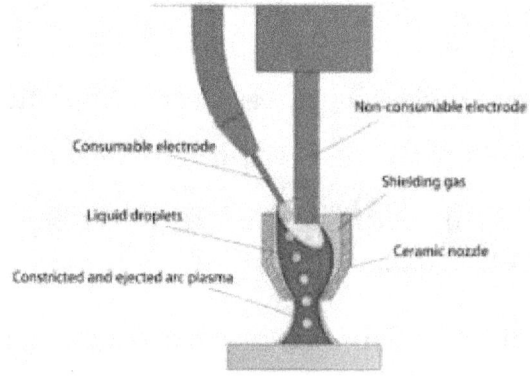

Consumables – This term refers to parts of the torch that are eroded during basic cutting operations.

Crack – This is a fracture type with a sharp tip and an opening that possess a usual high ratio of length and width in the metal.

Defect – This refers to natural discontinuities in a metal. It also involves accumulated and unattractive effects in a metal that could cause a project to be rejected.

Deposited Metal – During the welding and sometimes soldering process, the added filler metal is referred to as deposited metal.

Distortion – Change in shape of a welded structure.

Ductility – Ability or flexibility rate of a material that allows it to be permanently deformed.

Edge Preparation – This is the preparation of the base metal edges of a metal by cutting, cleaning and plating of the individual joint members.

Elastic Limit – Elastic limit is the highest level of stress a material can experience without being permanently deformed.

Elasticity – The innate ability of a base metal to go back to its original shape after it has been deformed.

Electrode – This is the plasma arc torch part that emits arc current.

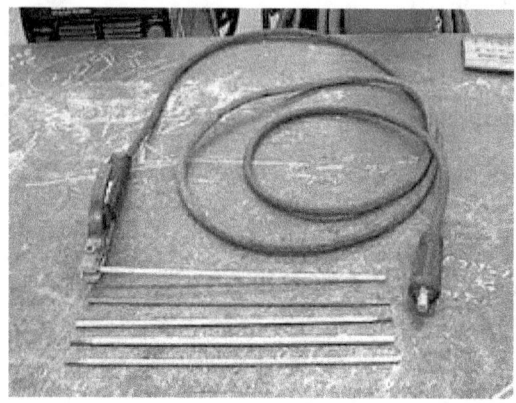

Electrode Coating – This the mixture of minerals that is placed on the core wire. Other chemicals and metallic alloys are also applied.

Electron – Particles with a negative charge that revolves around the nucleus in an atom that is positively charged.

Element – This refers to an ultimate substance, which cannot be broken down into other substances.

Face – An important part of the weld bead located between the "toes."

Filler Metal – This is the metal that is added in the welding process.

Filler Wire – This is similar to the filler metal and it refers to a spooled wire.

Fillet Weld – This has a cross-section like that of a triangle that joins two separate surfaces at opposite surfaces at right angles to each other in a lap joint, T-joint, or corner joint.

Flux – This is a tool used to reduce the spatter and contribute to welding bead shapes. The flux can also act as a cleaning agent used during arc welding to dissolve oxides and release trapped gases and slag. They help make the weld metal neat by floating impurities to the surface where they can be solidified and form slag covering.

Forging – This is the act of deforming a metal into a new shape through a very strong compressive force.

Fumes – An airborne solid generated by welding or cutting. They are usually sub-micron and airborne as they move with the air currents.

Fusion – Melting and joining of filler and base metal to produce a weld.

Porosity – The presence of gas pockets in a metallic solid, and it is usually scattered.

Preheating – The heating of base metal before the welding process fully begins to reduce the thermal shock and cooling rate.

Quench / Quenching – A process of cooling metals or steel quickly through hardening and quenching through air, oil, and water.

Shield / Shielding Gas – This is an unusual type of gas referred to as secondary gas, unlike plasma gas. It doesn't pass through the nozzle's orifice. A shield is formed around the arc just as it passes around the nozzle.

Slag – This is the brittle mass that builds a form over the weld bead on coated welds. It is also formed during slag-producing welding processes like flux-cored electrodes, submerged arc welding. When a weld is made with gas metal or tungsten arc, it is slag-free.

Spatter – A reinforcement resulting from the welding process that pours on the other side from which the welding is done.

Spray Arc Welding – In this welding process, there is transfer in the form of small droplets of molten material.

Steel – A term used to refer to any alloy of iron that contains up to 1.4% carbon.

Strain – This is the result of stressing the metal. The features are extreme stretches or deformation of the material.

Stub – This is the short remaining iron or electrode after the welding process.

Stress – A great amount of force applied to a metal that threatens to break or deform it.

Tensile Strength – Firm resistance of a base metal to a strong force that can pull it apart.

Throat – The part of the orifice with a cylindrical shape that is in control of the quantity of oxygen consumable.

T-Joint – A joint, where to individual, is approximately located at a right-angle position opposite each other to make the shape T.

Ultimate tensile strength – This is the maximum force applied to the material that enables it to pass through subjection without failure.

Undercut – This occurs when a groove melts into the base metal that is yet to be unfilled by the weld metal and is positioned to the adjacent location to the toe of the weld.

Work Hardening – The capacity of a workpiece to become hardened due to cold rolling, cold working, or other deformation processes like bending or drawing.

Workpiece – This term is used to describe a piece of metal to be welded or gouged.

Chapter 3

Welding Tips and Tricks

1. Before you start, prepare the machine, your tools, and your metals. This will guarantee your efficiency and productivity to a very large extent.

2. Practice how to handle the gun without welding. Position your hand on the barrel and use the other hand to pull the trigger of the gun. Maintain a comfortable position that will allow you to move the gun over the workpiece steadily. Make conscious and consistent practice using the same enthusiasm you are likely to use when it is a serious project. You can also purchase metals and other tools to make it real before you do a very serious project.

3. Touch the wire on the surface very lightly, take a squeeze at the trigger and pull the gun gently in your direction before you start welding.

4. Do a practice run as many times as possible, especially as a beginner. Do a lot of tests running before you make your first weld; it will boost your confidence.

5. Always have spare tools or electrodes prepared by the side, if you can afford it. You wouldn't want to realize halfway into your project that a particular tool is missing.

6. Electrification is a common hazard that could happen when using an electric welder. The situation could worsen if you happen to touch any part of the electrode circuit while touching the base metal. You are exposed to this danger of electric shock if you weld in wet areas, wear damp cloth while working, weld on a metal floor, and weld in an awkwardly cramped condition of kneeling or lying.

7. Protect yourself from burns and electrification by wearing safety clothes.

8. Expose yourself to good training. With good training, you will be safe from unnecessary dangers and be well equipped with standard knowledge on making exquisite projects.

9. Keep away flammables from your workspace; they are susceptible to fire. Having flammable in your workshop could make it explosive and pose great danger to you. They should be as far from there as possible. Excessive sparks, heat, or splatters generated in the welding process can set the whole place ablaze.

10. When dealing with painted metal, you have to be conscious of the disadvantage the paint poses to your weld. It can produce toxic fumes that are going to be unsafe for you to inhale. Also, it will prevent the metal from giving penetration to the weld. You won't also be able to strike an arc with the welder. You will have to use an angle grinder

to grind the surface of the area you intend to weld.

11. Undoing welds without a grinder. If you want to break welds without using a grinder, you must use a bandsaw and handsaw or use the thermal process. Here are the basic steps to follow; mark the part of the metal you want to cut using a pencil, clamp the metals, turn on the compressor or gas you are using and adjust the flame of the torch, so it is focused on the weld. Then move your tool slowly along the marked line you have made. You can leave the metals to cool after you have turned off the tools.

12. How to make the weave welding technique pattern using MIG. These weaves are used for wider welds that range from tight to side motion, where a stranger bead is used to make welds that are big and wide enough for a single pass. Weaves are used for large joints without distortion issues. This formula allows heat at a

particular travel speed that eliminates weaves from critical joints.

13. Assess weld joints and check for excessive gaps. If there is any, clamp the part in the right position. Wrong joints or positioning can lead to uncontrollable issues like burn-through and distortion, especially if you are using TIG.

14. To solve cracks, apply heat on both sides of the joint to have the right temperature. Then clamp the metals together. Before you start welding, run a little check on your machine settings.

15. How to make the whipping welding technique pattern. This doesn't work on all joints like the circle pattern; it is majorly used on joints with fillet beads. It preheats the joint before adding the filler metal while retaining the puddle in a tight range. This pattern is good for beginner welders as it allows them to control their travel speed. This pattern involves taking two steps backward

and one backward. It is just like walking and putting one foot in front of the other.

16. How to make the steady motion patterns using MIG. This is the most basic technique and it requires the welder to be set exactly as needed. This pattern comes down to electrode angle, travel speed, and machine settings; it produces a perfect weld at just any motion. Robots also use it.

17. How to make the circle welding technique pattern. This is a medium pattern between the whipping and weaves technique pattern; it works well on joints and can be applied almost everywhere. To use this pattern, make a small circle, go forward and repeat the circle; you can repeat this as many times as you wish.

18. Some processes require manual input on the welder; the modern process is being carried out by a robot. When it is performed by a robot, the

process is tagged as automatic welding. TIG provides semiautomatic welding and automatic welding, unlike other techniques or welders, which are mostly manual.

19. Place the filler rod under the gas shroud to prevent it from oxidizing and to keep it warm.

20. To bring about a total fusion, remove weld and base metal from the welded joint to bring about the root.

Chapter 4

Getting Started With Welding

Tools and Supplies

Metal

Metal is one of the most important things to be considered in welding. It cannot be accorded the most important position because all tools that will be discussed are also important, but some are more relevant in use than others.

Metals are made up of different elements; this is why you must choose your metals carefully. The elements in the metals affect their color, texture and stability. You need to be able to assert the properties of the metal you intend to weld into account. This is also because every metal responds to heat differently and can be manipulated in unique ways that are peculiar to them. They all respond differently to the different types of welding methods that are being used.

Here is a brief list of the checks to make when selecting a metal;

- Melting point: this is unique according to the elements in the metal.
- Ductility: it refers to how metal reacts to bending and stretching.
- Electrical conductivity: this affects what the metal can be used for, the volume or amount of heat it can be used to conduct.
- Strength: the ability the metal has to withstand pressure. It analyses the breaking point of a metal.

There are six main types of metals, although there are more that are not in record.

The common six are;

Aluminum

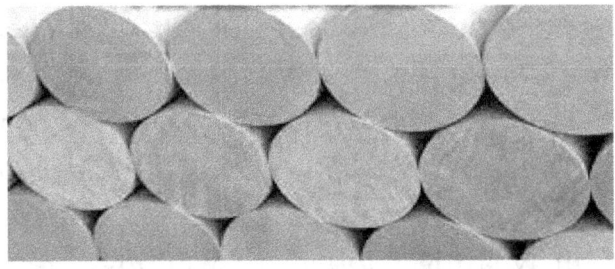

This metal is used in a large number of industrial applications and it produces really high corrosion resistance as well as good electrical conduction. This metal is really light, and it is very easy to carry around from place to place. It is soft and easy to weld, especially when the proper techniques. It includes copper/ aluminum alloy, manganese alloy and zinc alloy. The method used in welding aluminum is the TIG welding (GTAW) and GMAW (gas metal arc welding). Aluminum has little or no clarification, and it is liable to porosity, stress corrosion cracking, and hot cracking. You have to be careful when dealing with metals to prevent burns caused by certain aluminum alloys that have a very simple melting.

Copper

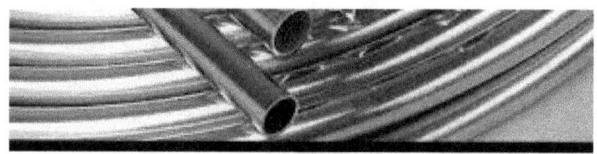

Copper is popular because of its high electrical conductivity, heat conductivity, corrosion resistance, wear-resistance and appearance. Every copper has at least 99.3% copper content, some contain more, but that's the minimum copper content. The processes followed in welding copper are welding, brazing and soldering, and it is finished. There are several types of copper alloys; copper nickel-zinc (also called nickel silver), copper-nickel, copper silicon (also called silicon bronze), aluminum bronze, copper-tin, brass (also called copper-zinc), and 5% high copper alloys.

Gas Tungsten Arc Welding (TIG) and Gas Metal Arc Welding are two methods used in welding copper. Manual metal welding is a bad option as it can result in poor quality.

Cast Iron

This refers to very thick and hard material with great carbon and silicon content. Due to its hardness, it could be difficult to work with the cast iron as it can be quite difficult to control. Its hardness could translate into minimal malleability and ductility. The main problem with the cast iron is its tendency to crack due to its unmalleability. The cracks, if they eventually occur, can be filed or grinded. It would take a well-trained welder to reduce the cracks by properly preheating them. Before welding with cast iron, the surface of the iron has to be cleaned to eliminate every ingrained oil and grease. The cast iron is usually welded with oxyacetylene welding.

Magnesium

This is a lighter version of aluminum. It actually weighs 2/3 of aluminum. It also absorbs vibration, which makes it very easy to cast. It uses the same method used in welding aluminum. The only difference is its melting temperature. It is usually welded with a Tig welder. Note that magnesium's shavings from its grinding are highly flammable, use a gas shield if you must grind magnesium and don't try to use water to put out the flames.

Stainless Steel

This type of steel is multipurpose, especially in the industry. It is known for its high strength and corrosion resistance characteristics, unlike carbon steel. The corrosion resistance is achieved by adding 10% to 30% chromium to nickel alloy, iron and other elements. It also has a very low melting point that causes it to melt before others in the face of heat. Hence, you have to be moderate when applying heat to a thing. Stainless steel still can expand and it retains its susceptibility to temperature. There is a need to consider all these points and factors to avoid thermal stress and cracking. The major downside is its high cost.

Carbon Steel

Steel contains very strong elements in itself independently. Steel as an alloy possesses irons and 2% of other elements. Carbon steel is quite a popular metal and can be found in high, low and medium varieties. The higher the carbon content, the stronger the steel. Before welding, endeavor to clean the welding areas, as it tends to rust and flake.

Welders

There are seven major types of welders

1. TIG-Gas Tungsten Arc Welding (GTAW)

These two names are used to describe the same welder. Whether it is addressed as TIG or GTAW, they all refer to the same thing. It is made of tungsten and has a none consumable electrode. The TIG is one of those types of welding that doesn't require filler metal. The two metals that are being joined together are well sufficient. It is necessary to use a gas tank with the TIG welding; it helps to provide a constant gas flow to protect the weld. Hence, it is necessary that the TIG welding is done indoors, away from external elements. TIG welding defines a form of welding that creates appealing welds but doesn't bring about a splatter. It is mostly reserved for experienced welders; if you try this without experience, you would have many difficulties.

2. MIG Welding

Many persons tend to argue how simple this form of welding is. However, it remains the best welder that new welders can use. MIG in full is Metal Inert Gas, and it is also called Gas Metal Arc Welding (GMAW). When this process is analyzed, it involves feeding the filler metal through the machine wand. You have to be wary of external elements interfering with this gas; you are to shield it from external elements by spraying gas around it. You can only use this welder indoors. Using it outdoors will expose it more to external elements. You can weld virtually all the types of metals on this welder at different levels of thickness using the regulator.

The filler metal that is used here is a consumable wire passed through a spool. It is also used as an electrode. The wire is passed through the wand continuously, and it allows you to dial at a perfect speed, after which an arc is created around the tip of the wire and the base metal. It is positioned in a place where it can easily melt. After it melts, it fills in the metal automatically.

If this process is coherently followed, you will definitely achieve a smooth, light and appealing weld.

3. Electron Beam Welding

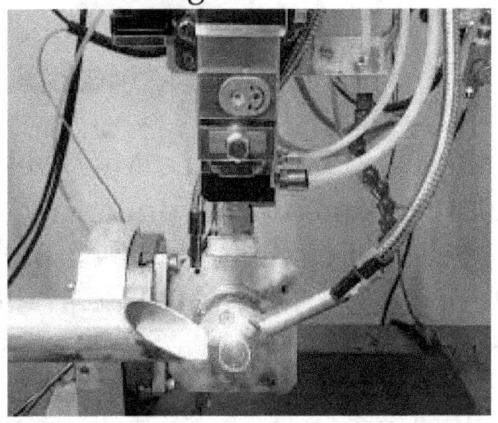

From the name electrons, you can tell that this is a unique and unusual type of weld. It builds electron beams of very high velocity. These electrons generate serious heat when welding through kinetic or active energy. Only experienced welders can handle this sophisticated type of welder as it is basically performed by a machine in a vacuum.

4. Flux-cored Arc Welding (FCAW)

This welder is similar to the MIG welder in the sense that it also performs double duty. First of all, you would have to fill in the electrode, which has a flux core just around the weld. This flux helps to build a gas shield and eliminated the need to get an external gas.

This welder produces high heat; therefore, it is best used for building and repairing thick and heavy metals. Most welders use it to repair heavy equipment. It is highly conservative as it gives the right pressure of heat to the metal. However, you would need to do a little clean-up after welding to make a nicely finished weld.

5. Stick Shielded Metal Arc Welding (SMAW)

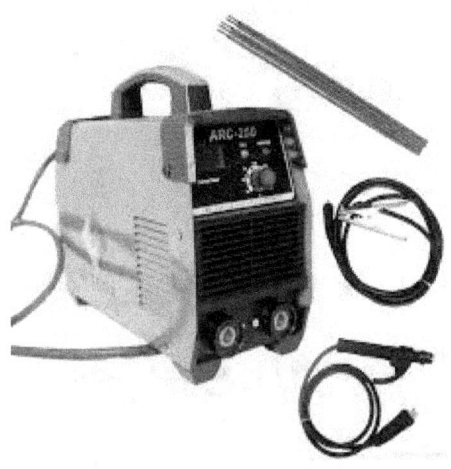

This type of welder was first found in 1930 and has passed through several years of improvement and updated up till now. Unlike other sophisticated machines that are majorly for experienced professionals, the SMAW is easy to learn and simple to handle, and it is also cheaper to operate. This makes it a good choice for beginners. However, it could get messy when it splatters; thorough clean-up is usually required after every weld.

As the name suggests, the stick in this name refers to the filler metal added when welding. This stick is also termed a 'replaceable electrode stick.' To connect this stick to the metal effectively, an arc is built that allows the electrode to melt into the filler metal and finally create the weld. The stick is usually flux-coated. As it is heated up, it develops a gas cloud that helps prevent the metal's exposure to oxidation.

When it cools, gas happens to settle on the metal and it becomes slag.

6. Electroslag

Electroslag is an advanced type of welding for professionals and experts in the field. It is majorly used in joining the thin edges of metal plates vertically. Unlike other welders where the weld is usually added to the metal's external part, with this metal, the weld is in the middle of the two metals. Consumable metal guile tube is used in feeding the filler metal. This filler metal for several years has been the copper electrode wire. Electricity is first introduced, then an arc is formed and the weld starts forming from the down part of the seam and slowly moves to the top, creating a thick weld in the place of the seam. This is a top automated machine.

7. Plasma Arc Welder

This welder has a similar form to the GTAW. However, it is a much smaller machine. This welder possesses a torch that is quite different from the other torches and produces much more temperature. To create plasma, pressure is applied on the gas into the wand. After the plasma has been created, it is ionized so that it can be electrically conductive. In this condition, the arc is created and fashioned until it produces very high temperatures that can melt the base metal you are welding. You have the chance to increase the welding speed. This welder allows for deep weld penetration and provides a very deep level of strength.

Welding Wire

The welding wire is a tool used in fusing two base metals together. In a more explanatory sense, the welding wire refers to a slim metal that is used to facilitate a heated arc by joining two metals together. It is usually hammered or compressed under a heat source. That is how the

There are three types of welding wires. They are all important in themselves. However, you can't use all the types of welding wires. Each of these wires is for specific machines.

1. Solid gas metal arc welding wire: this wire is majorly used in the metal arc welder. GMAW requires a solid wire electrode that has the potential to secure the weld from gas. This thing rod fills in that purpose just perfectly. This kind of wire is specifically used in short arc procedures on thin materials. You might have to increase the pulse-welding deposition rates. Also, it is the cleanest wire to use as it doesn't leave splatters.

However, it doesn't handle mill scale and contaminants well. If you perceive your work surface is dirty, make sure to deoxidize the wire heavily.
2. Gas shielded flux cored arc welding wire: this core wire is deoxidized and fluxed with a deoxidization agent from the environment. It can be engineered in a way that tends the mechanical properties of the deposit. This wire tolerates dirty base metals most. This wire also encourages speed, and this wire is the best choice in allowing high deposition. The FCAW requires most clean-up because due to the leftover slag on the weld.
3. Composite GMAW (metal corded) wire: these wires have metallic components in their core. It is as tough and clean as the solid GMAW wire. They also tolerate dirty base metals but not as the flux-cored wire. The corded wire helps make speedy welds and can be used on thin materials using a short arc procedure. Asides from good speed, the wires also provide strength and mechanical properties. The components of the core usually influence its mechanical properties.

Shielding Gas

This is a gas that is commonly used in welding. They refer to inert gases that are used in gas metal arc welding. The shielding gases is used to prevent oxygen and water vapor. The shielding gas reduces the quality of the weld, and sometimes, it could also make it stronger. The shielding gas also shields from the environment that can contaminate the metal. Improper choice of welding gas can lead to a splatter.

There are two main categories of shielding gases

Inert and semi-inert gases

The inert gases are majorly used in gas tungsten arc welding and non-ferrous metals. The semi-inert shielding gases include oxygen, hydrogen, nitrogen, carbon dioxide. They are mainly used on ferrous metals with the GMAW welder.

Endeavor to use these gases in small quantities; when used in large quantities, they can damage the weld. However, if it is appropriately used, it improves the weld characteristics. Shielding gasses are used to provide the desired bead shape and reduce splatter. It also helps to encourage fusion during welding.

Welding Table

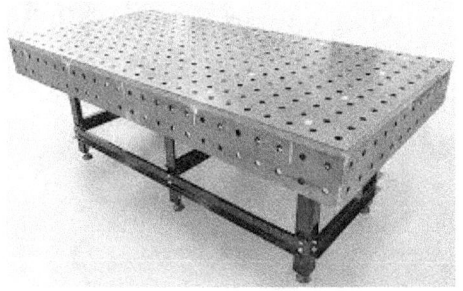

The welding table is a platform or a flat surface where the metal is placed for fabrication during welding. It is also viewed as a workbench for many reasons. This is one tool you can't do without while welding; you will need a surface to make your cuts and a place to work. The welding table gives you a stable and firm surface to place your work. It also provides you assistance during measuring on squaring. Make sure to invest money to get a high-quality welding table; this will improve the safety of your workplace and sharpen your efficiency. There are welding tables of different sizes, shapes, heights, and designs. Another set of distinguishing factors is the material and table size. Welding tables could come in various materials like iron, square, and carbon/steel. Wood is not an option as it is susceptible to fire hazards.

When selecting based on table size, consider the width of the table and the allowance it gives you to make cuts of specific sizes. Also, consider the available workspace.

Welding Clamps

Here is a top must-have. Some professionals would admonish you to get at least 10 welding clamps. You might have bigger projects and need to tack several parts of your workpiece in place; how would you hold them down? Here is where the clamp comes in. without these clamps, your welding could go loose on the weld and your project could get out of square. Here is an order to follow when using a clamp, cut your pieces to length, fit the pieces tightly together, clamp them, tack-weld, remove clamps, lay the final welds.

C Clamp

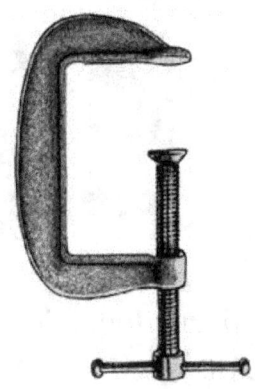

It is preached that you have an assortment of C clamps to save yourself from frustrations. You need the C clamp to secure your work firmly to the table while you cut or make other processes on the metal. Don't mix up the importance of the welding clamp and the C clamp. The C-clamp is majorly used to keep the metal fixed to the work surface, while the Welding clamp is used in holding two base metals together after they have been clamped.

Oxy-Acetylene Setup

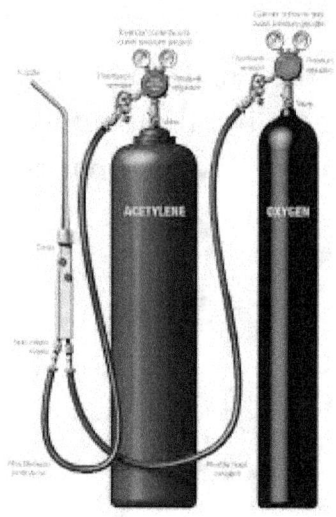

This tool is very multifunctional. You can use it to make welds, bend with it, make cuts with it, and many other things. It is a multipurpose tool everyone using the oxy-acetylene technique should have. With this setup, you can make unique or complex shapes like a circle, not just a nay circle but also a perfect circle. You can also make an accurate 90 degrees bend, amongst other things.

Angle Grinder

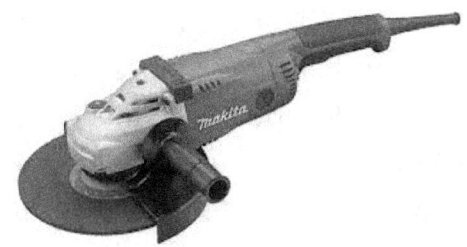

Here is another top necessity in your toolbox. The grinder is used to smooth out your projects, especially at the end; it is best for big projects and could be quite too much on small projects or base metals. The file can stand in its place for smaller metals. They can also be used for precise cutting.

Wire Brush

It is popularly known as the metal brush, and you will need this tool if you are into a welding type that creates slag. If you are using the stick welder, scrape off the slag gathered on the surface to fully reveal the weld. A chipping hammer could also be used in place of the metal brush for this same task. The slag coating usually forms during the process of welding.

Sheet Welding Gauge

For some projects, it might be required that you use a metal of a particular weight. Also, some welders define the limit of metal thickness that the weld can accommodate, so you would have to check your base metals' thickness and weight before you start welding. You just have to slide your welding gauge's openings over your workpiece; the gauge will feed you the result. It is not really a must-have tool for beginners, but you might have a lot of metals lying around that you need to combine for a project. To ascertain their compatibility, you might need to gauge them.

Speed Square

This tool shouldn't be missing in your toolbox for no reason. The speed square is a very necessary tool that helps you achieve 90 degrees angle when working on a huge metal. Here is how you use it; if you happen to be working on a metal 12 inches, you have to set the metal's speed square. Mark the measurement on the surface of the metal. To make 45 degrees, you just need to slide your speed square until you hit the 45 mark. This is a very basic tool you need if you are to achieve a perfect angle on your metal.

Chop Saw

The chop saw isn't really a required tool for beginners to have in their workshop, but it is important because it ensures you produce clean cuts. You would be making many cuts in the workshop; you need to have a saw to serve such purpose any day or time. Once in a while, you might have a dull blade, but you could always replace it.

Tape Measure

This is a common measuring tool used to measure the length of hard materials like wood, metal, and others. The design makes it easy to be carried in a pocket or toolkit. Today, it is even more portable. This is a metallic rule that is used to measure the metal before it is cut.

Slag Hammer

It is also called a chipping hammer, and it is used to chip away slag coating after welding to uncover the weld hidden under the slag.

Welding Torch

This is an automatic system to coordinate the welding electrode to the arc center. To weld the welding power to the electrode, there is a need to provide a shielding area for the arc. In simple terms, the welding torch is used to provide access to the weld.

MIG Pliers

You would remember that I stated the MIG as the best welder for beginners. Now it is also very important for beginners to use the MIG pliers. If you would use the welder, you must certainly use the plier. You need not fear; they are very easy to use and have several important functions they perform that can help your welding process become easier. They help you remove hot gun nozzle. This nuzzle is usually very hot, so you need a tool you remove; a gloved hand is not an option.

Soapstone

This is a marking tool used to indent a mark on metal when preparing metals before welding. It also helps you to withstand high welding heat. There are also available markers that will help you achieve the exact same result. It is just like the tailor's chalk. If you intend to cut out a particular shape from metal, you just need to draw the shape on the metal using the soapstone and make the cut.

Metal File

You must be familiar with nail files. There are some metal blares that you tend to cause when you start cutting your projects. To clean them off, you need to use the file. Grinders are used for bigger projects; files are mostly used for small projects. They are such a great investment and you should be interested in knowing that they are very affordable.

Helmet

This is a basic safety and important tool you need to have in your store. It secures your eyes from the splatter and injury of the flame. It also gives you a focused vision of the weld. When selecting a helmet, ensure to go for an auto-darkening welding helmet. This will help reduce the brightness of the fire from the welding process, and it won't be focused on your eyes. A silent option is to buy a solid-shaped welding helmet, but it won't help you. It would limit your vision and frustrate you in some sense. You would not be able to see your workpiece well. The auto-darkening helmet is the best there is for you to use, as it helps you focus your vision properly.

Safety Glasses

When using tools like angle grinders, you need to have your eyes protected with some safety shields. This will preserve your eyes from the sparks that would be flying around in the workshop. Those sparks are usually small metals that could blind you if they happen to get in contact with your eyes, so don't take chances; get a safety glasses or a grinding face shield.

Gloves

Here is another safety tool. Gloves help you protect your hands. There are very thick gloves that you could use in picking up pieces of metal without endangering your hands. This is most preferably prescribed for beginners. Thin leather gloves are a very good option to help you achieve a great firm hold on the metal. However, you could have both thin and thick gloves in your closet; they will do you great good. Nonetheless, your glove might not protect you totally from heat; the temperature of the arc is usually around 10,000 degrees. So, you are not totally immune to heat because you are putting on gloves.

Welding Magnets

These are special welding tools used in fabricating a metal. Using these magnets, you can successfully hold the two base metals and create a 90-degree angle in any of your welding projects. You could use this tool when you build weld frames for tables, fire pit grates, and a lot more. They are mostly used in small projects as they come in mostly small sizes. If you want to use it for a large project, you have to buy many magnets. For a square frame, you would need to place one magnet on each side of the workpiece to hold it firmly in place.

Welding Framing Jig

This is not commonly used by beginners; however, it would help you create perfect square frames if you understand the jig's use. It is a simple fabrication tool anyone can handle.

To use this tool, insert two pieces of your work into the jig, make tack welds, and tighten it. That will give you a 90-degree angle.

Setting Up Your Welding Workshop

Having a workshop in your home is very exquisite and comfortable. To build a workshop, there are many basic things that you need to know. First of all, you need to understand that for you to grow a career in welding successfully, there are systems you ought to put in place. Sometimes you encrypt that system by setting up a place where you can establish your materials.

The welding process can be quite rough; hence, some of the tools are very crude, and you can't do them just anywhere.

You can set up your workshop in a garage, outdoors, a storage space, or the backyard.

In choosing any of these locations to situate your workshop, you have to put in consideration the following points:

- Ease of accessibility
- Safety
- Weather
- Space area

After analyzing these factors and then deciding which work area is best for you, you have to start gathering the instruments or tools you'd need to set up a great workshop.

This guide is specifically for building a workshop in your backyard. Here is the basic equipment you'll need to have a good setup.

- Metal welding table (preferably solid metal)
- TIG Welder and any other welder
- Electric power source
- Welding Clamps
- Angle Grinder
- Wire Brush
- Measure tape
- Fire extinguisher for safety

- Safety and protective wear

This is not a limitation to adding other equipment to your workshop. As the complexity of your workshop increases, the more equipment you add to your workshop.

Basic things to consider

Foundation: Irrespective of the location you choose for your welding workshop. You have to pay attention to the foundation.

Indoor shops have smooth flooring, unlike other workshops.

When you happen to be welding outdoor, be careful of positioning your work equipment near the grass as it could result in a serious fire incident.

If you are considering outdoor as your selection, you have to pour some concrete slab on the floor to avoid the risk of slipping.

This slab also gives you a firm surface that hides discoloration and possible stains. The rush to get things done will be reduced to the barest minimum.

Climate: One thing worthy of concern is that welding in open air can be nice as it guarantees ventilation but could also have its downside. Your work is exposed to humidity, harsh temperature and dirt. You would need a very strong shielding gas to shield your metal from these contaminants. Find a metal or welding technique that fits the project you are carrying out. Also, you have to consider the safety of the work place. When you use indoor shops to make welds, you can easily clear out the wood shavings and have a clean floor, but when outdoors, the shavings accumulate and could be a problem in the long run. They could cause harm to the bare feet and paws.

If you are considering welding outside, pour a concrete slab on the floor designed for outdoor work, this will protect you from impending dangers caused by the roughness of the outdoor.

Also, you should consider your tools; welding materials aren't cheap in any way; hence you have to be careful about the kind of climate condition you expose them to.

Techniques

The best technique for outdoor use is the MIG and SMAW welding technique. This is because the shielding gas is produced very close to the weld pool. Stick or SMAW is the most commonly used outdoor technique. The TIG's shielding gas is more susceptible to external elements.

Putting tarps or fireproof materials is one way to shield your welding station from disastrous wind that can push away the shielding gases. Welding curtains are also another good option to be considered in protecting the weld station and the welder from harmful arc flash and radiation.

If you intend to use an outdoor space permanently or long term, you should consider adding fixtures that will enable you to store tools and make welding way easier. You should also consider redressing the walls. However, this stress isn't necessary if you don't intend to stay long outdoor.

Metals

This is another thing that is worthy of consideration, some metals like aluminum are very sensitive to pollutants. If welded in the open, the possibility that it gets contaminated is very high. These contaminants could refer to dust, dirt, and pollen. If you are welding outdoor, you should replace weak metals like aluminum with more stable metals like steel. Also, ensure to be extra careful during the welding process not to initiate contaminants on yourself.

Storage

The welding tools are really susceptible to damages; the welding equipment should be stored aright if it will last longer. Building a storage area helps you keep them safe and ensure that they are easily retrievable.

Power source

Be keen on selecting a location that allows you access to power. Although, you can use extension cords to channel electricity to the location you are working.

Finally, convenience is the absolute checker. If all these things are met and there is no convenience, then you should consider another location.

Welding Hazards and Safety Precautions

Electric shock: During the welding process, at a stage, electric circuits tend to create a mass of molten metal, which could bring about electric shock. Compared with all the possible hazards in welding, electric shock is one of the most hazardous dangers welders are exposed to. It can result in very serious injuries and fatalities that could cause dysfunction in the body. The shock could cause you to fall from a height or have even more terrible injuries, depending on your standing position.

Noise hazards: Welding could be such a noisy activity, especially from 100dB(A) noise level, which is above the average loud noise level of 85dB(A). This can lead to massive ear pain and eventually result in impairment if not well managed. Hearing loss could be facilitated into tinnitus, also known as the ringing of the ear. It could also result in vertigo, also understood as occasional dizziness. It could also increase blood pressure.

Burns: Burns can be caused by high temperature, contact with molten metals, UV rays and other factors. The burns are always severe, depending on the area it affects. Burns are the commonest of the hazards and the easier to prevent. However, many welders become a victim as a result of their carelessness or oversight.

Exposure to fumes or gases: This could affect all of the senses. Normally the welder is exposed to very dangerous fumes. In fact, that is what he uses to work. These gases are dangerous and produce very harmful fumes that are swallowed into the lungs. Depending on the type of gas and the duration of exposure, the damage might be severe. Possible damages are pneumonia, occasional asthma, lung cancer, and metal fume fever. All these things are a result of accumulative lung irritation.

Here is a list of precautions that could save you the stress of having to face the above-mentioned hazards.

1. Get a PPE (Personal Protective Equipment): This includes in its fullness-welding helmets with a side shield. The helmet protects the face from UV radiation, particles, burns, hot slag and many other facial or eye hazards. When selecting a side shield, ensure to go for the right lens size for the type of work you intend to do. Also, before use, make sure that the manufacturer's guidelines are followed and the lens is adjusted until it gives you a good fit. Also, make use of a fire-resistant hood under the helmet to protect the hind of your head.
2. Respirators: A comfortable respirator will be easy for you to carry around. It also protects you from fumes and oxides that the welding process is bound to create.

3. Fire resistant clothing: This will majorly help you to avoid burns. This clothing has the ability to protect you from heat, fire, and radiation created during the welding process. It should be a simple attire without pockets, cuffs. If there must be pockets, do well to cover it with flaps or taped closed. Avoid using synthetic clothing; the best material to use is leather.
4. Ear protection: You can use fire-resistant ear muffs to protect your ears from alarming noise.
5. Boots and gloves: Your boots and gloves must be made of rubber. This way, they get to shield you from electric shocks, heat fire, falling objects, and burns.
6. Receive appropriate training: You have to be part of a training before establishing your career in welding. Adequate training will educate you on the basics and fundamental information you need to start professional welding.
7. Ensure that your workspace is ventilated: You need ventilation to work well in the workshop. You can't work well if the room is choky; it is dangerous to your health and could endanger you the more. Remember, welding has to do with

a lot of heat, so you need an opening to help you cool down the room from the heat. You also need ventilation to combat the pollutants gathered from the welding process. You might have to consider using respirators if you still don't feel conducive in the atmosphere.

Welding Positions and Joints

Welding Positions

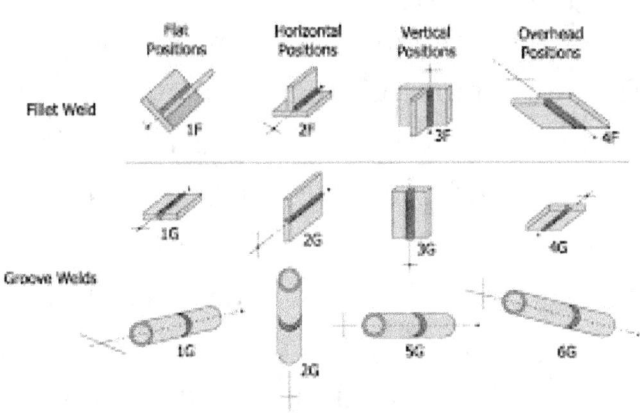

There are four basic welding positions: the flat, horizontal, vertical, and overhead positions. Before we launch into analyzing these positions, their uniqueness and how they are important, let's do a little rundown on what welding positions are.

In simple words, welding position is the position of the welder in relation to the workpiece.

The main four types of welding positions are discussed extensively below.

1. Flat position: Also called downward position, it is the easiest and commonest form of welding. In fact, it is the first position beginners tend to learn when learning to position, as it is very basic. In this position type, the metals are placed flat to allow the welder to pass an electric arc over it. This arc is moved across the metal in a horizontal manner. The top side of the materials is fused together and welded so that the molten metal moves downward into its edges.
2. Horizontal position: It is also referred to as an out-of-position weld. This position can be quite challenging for beginners as it requires specific complex skills to perform. The axis of welding this metal is usually horizontal. The position the project eventually takes depends on the weld, and the weld bead is placed at a position where

the vertical and horizontal piece of metal joins at a 90-degree angle. If you are performing a groove weld, the weld's face will be on a vertical plane.
3. Vertical position: For the vertical position, the weld and the plate will be placed vertically. The major problem facing welders using this position is that the molten metal flows downward and piles up there. To prevent this issue, you would have to weld in an uphill or downward position.
4. Overhead: This is the most technical position to work on, and mostly professionals use it. This welding is performed with the two base metals above the welder. To perform this position effectively, the welder will have to angle himself alongside the equipment to make the joints. The possible downside of this position is metal sagging. When the metal sags, it forms a crown-like shape. To prevent such a situation, the puddle of molten metal should be small.

Welding Joints

Types of Welding Joints

- Butt Joint
- Lap Joint
- Corner Joint
- Edge Joint
- Tee Joint

This is very different from the weld's position; it refers, in particular, to the location where base pieces of metal are joined together. It also refers to how metals are joined. There are five majorly used weld joints.

1. Butt joints: Two pieces of metal are joined using their edges in the same plane. This is the commonest type of fabrication that is used in fabricating structures and piping systems. It is very simple to prepare because it has flexible options to achieve the same desired results. Butt joints can be done in various ways and each serves its own purposes. The varying factors of these options in the butt joints include the shape of the gap's groove and width. Here are some examples of the butt joints;

- Square
- Single bevel
- Double bevel
- Single J
- Double J
- Single V
- Double V
- Single U
- Double U grooves

The metal's surface that gets melted in the process of welding is addressed as the faying surface. This faying surface is usually shaped before the welding process to increase the strength of the weld. This process of increasing the weld's strength is called edge preparation. You have to prepare the faying surfaces for welding in the butt joint because of the metals.

When making a groove, sometimes, the shape, size and angle of the metal can be specified. Most especially, if the exact dimensions are unknown, the groove can be made to the necessary size. Note that the wider you groove, the more welding you would have to implement.

2. Lap joints: Two pieces of metal lap each other partially. This is a modified version of the butt joint. It is formed when two base metals are placed in a manner where they are overlapping one another. Welds can be made on any side as this joint is used in welding metals of differing thicknesses.

   The Lap joints are not used on thick materials as they are mostly used for sheet metal. The major downside of this joint is corrosion due to overlapping material. Nonetheless, you can correct this by using modifying variables or good techniques where necessary.

3. T joints: This occurs when two pieces are joined centrally at the right angle such that it forms a T shape. These joints are usually likened to a type of filet weld, and it is mostly formed when a tube or pipe is being welded onto a base plate.

   To achieve penetration with this type of weld, the welder has to guarantee that there is successful penetration of the roof into the weld. Below is a list of the styles that are used in creating a Tee joint:

- Plug weld
- Slot weld
- Bevel-groove weld
- Fillet weld
- J-groove weld
- Melt-through weld
- Flare-bevel-groove weld

These joints are hardly ever prepared with groove until the base metal is not usually prepared with groove, unless the base metal is thick, and both sides cannot withstand the joint's load to support. One popular defect with the Tee joint is lamellar tearing. It is usually caused by restrictions the joint experiences. Welders commonly create a stopper to prevent all forms of joint deformities.

4. Corner joints: this is where the two base metals are fused exactly at a 90-degree angle. Corner joints are very similar to the T welding joints. The sharp difference is just the position of the metal hen making the joints. Unlike the T joint, which is placed in the middle, the corner joints are placed at the corner in either an open or

closed manner resulting in it forming an 'L' shape. They are the most common among the joints used in making basic products like table, chair, boxes, and other things.

5. **Edge joints:** These joints occur when the flat surfaces of the base metals are welded together. Weld joints are made to effectively align separate parts of metal together to distribute stresses evenly. There are a few forces that cause stress in joints weld. The strength and possibility for the edge joint to withstand forces depend on the design of the joint. Several joints are better at withstanding some types of forces than the others. The heat input rate, penetration, and deposition affect the welds used on specific joint designs. The following styles are used in edge joints:
    - U-groove
    - V-groove
    - J-groove
    - Corner-flange
    - Bevel-groove
    - Square-groove

- Edge-flange

Just like the lap joints, this joint is prone to corrosion. Slag inclusion, lack of fusion and porosity are also possible downsides of the edge joints.

Cleaning and Preparing Metal

Most times, metals are usually coated in grime and greasy. There could also be some rust flaking on the surface of the metal. As a beginner, you need to realize that surface preparation is a very important and uncompromised part of the welding progress. You have to clean your surface appropriately and get it well-prepped, if not, you might encounter a lot of problems eventually. You must learn how to deal with a multitude of surface issues; trust me they are a lot of them and you wouldn't want to be caught in the web of any of them.

How you prepare the metal surface for welding depends on the metal you would be using to work. Some metals contain a lot of grease that you can't but take out. You can easily take this out with a damp rag.

Asides from grease, you would also need to remove any rust or mill scale using an angle grinder. This rust could cause improper ground and lead to improper balance after welding.

Other commons surface issues are corrosion, rust, grime, or anything else that would make a difference and affect your project's outcome when you weld.

To prepare your surface, you need to simply start with the approach of cleaning your work surface with low VOC PRE or acetone.

These chemicals help to get rid of grease, stains, oil and other residues. A side warning is you have to be careful not to use this metal immediately after using the chemical on it as most at times, they tend to be flammable.

Some welders require that you use really clean metals on them, while some, like the MIG welder, don't really have a side effect on them. Some of these things have been discussed above. So, based on the type of welder you intend to use, you just have to discover how clean your metal has to be.

In some cases, cleaning a metal requires more than just wiping down the metal using a clean rag. Here is a list of steps to prepare metal for welding.

1. Wipe the surface using acetone
2. Clean out impurities and rust using an angle grinder, wire brush, abrasive blasting, and plasma cutter.
3. Use a sander or cleaner to clean the surface for a shiny/ rough look.
4. Finally, do a complete wipe down using an appropriate cleaner.

There are three commons situations you are likely to encounter when cleaning your metal surface.

1. Oily/ greasy surfaces
2. Painted/ coated surfaces
3. Rusty or abrasive surface

Undoing Welds

The welding process involves the fusing of metals together and you might make a wrong weld that you need to remove or undo, whichever case it is. Also, there are different kinds of weld, and some might require that undo a weld. When you make a weld, it happens to become stronger than even the metal itself. This means that you can't easily undo a weld, the same way you can easily undo a metal.

Here are methods to use in undoing a weld.

Thermal method

The word 'therm' refers to heat. This method categorically refers to the use of high temperature to undo welds. You can channel this high temperature through plasma cutters or oxy-acetylene torches.

Plasma cutting:

This involves using an accelerated jet of hot plasma to cut through electrical conductors. An arc is created using a direct current where the temperature can get up to 20,000 degrees Celsius; high-pressure airflow coming out of the small nozzle generates the required heat.

Per its cutting speed, plasma cutting can be beneficial because they are around five times faster compared to manual torches, cutting through several materials of different thicknesses; therefore, any deep welds can likewise be undone. They are also safe and easy to use without using flammable gases.

Torch cutting:

This is the use of acetylene torches, involving the combination of acetylene with oxygen to bring about flames of incredibly high temperature. This temperature is usually at 3500 degrees Celsius and it is used to weld or cut metals. It serves both purposes perfectly.

This method can be a little risky for beginners, as the two mixed gases can bring about a flame that is too hot and can injure the welder if not well handled.

To use this method, mark a line across where you want to make the cut and light up the torch. Carefully follow the marked line and make your cuts.

Mechanical method

This is the opposite or substitute for the thermal method. In the thermal method, the metal is cut through heat while in this method, the metal is cut manually. It involves cutting, grinding, or drilling.

Undoing welds manually without grinders:

You would have to drill or use the thermal reversal process.

Here are the processes to follow;

1. Mark the metal like in the thermal process
2. Secure the metal with a clamp

3. Turn on the compressor of your gas torch and adjust the flame of the torch
4. Move your tool slowly along the line you have marked.
5. After cutting, allow the metals to cool before using them.

Undoing welds using a circular saw or grinder:

Just as you can easily grind a weld bead down with an angle grinder, you can make cuts with this grinder. However, these cuts are not always as precise as plasma cutting, and it doesn't promote much heat. This is because there is not so much heat involved in this process; this process can't easily alter the base metal, and it cannot be used on really thick welds as well.

To use this method;

1. Mark the place in the metal where you want to make the cut
2. Secure the metal in a vice
3. Ensure to put on your protective gear; it is very necessary.
4. Connect your grinder to the power source
5. Slowly pass the metal through the grinder

6. After the cut, let the metal and grinder cool for a while before continuing your welding process.

Finishing Your Welds

The finishes used and the processes it requires are quite different and driven by the type of material you are using. This section focuses on carbon steel and stainless steel materials, respectively.

Finishing carbon steel vs. stainless steel

- In carbon steel, unfinished welds are usually stronger than finished welds; this is because finished welds involve a form of material removal through grinding.
- Finishing a weld with carbon steel is relatively easy and is usually painted.
- With carbon steel, the metal needs to be prepared to the extent where the paint can easily be applied, i.e., a rough surface will make the paint conform better compared to if the metal was properly finished to a shine.
- Stainless steel has more commercial applications than carbon steel.

- In stainless steel, a highly refined finish is used for its aesthetics. On the other hand, a handrail or elevator wall panel will need a No. 4 finish in disguising the visibility that is seen with scratches or fingerprints.
- In carbon steel, powder coating is usually used to color the metal, and a coarse-grained weld 2-step removal is good enough for this purpose.

Initial weld grinding

This process refers to the grinding down of the metal surface to remove excess stock from the concluded weld. This is done to reduce the weld bead to be equal with the parent metal. The craftsman can achieve this using an angle grinder with a simple grinding wheel.

This involves a high level of skill and experience, especially when using stainless steel. However, it can be used on all types of materials. The possible downside is gouging and undercutting, which could only occur in the metal worker's negligence. To avoid this, take good care to adopt the right angle when grinding.

Here are a few tips if you must use this method on carbon or stainless steel.

- This process is way easier on carbon steel and stainless steel.
- When working with a grinding wheel on stainless steel, a suitable product for it must be used, such as a disc blotter.
- To avoid creating noticeable spots on the stainless steel, grit with a medium grit after grinding down.
- To make your grinding more effective on the stainless steel, use the fiber disc or flap disc to work on the metal.
- During the forward and backward motion in carbon steel, apply constant pressure to achieve a sharp finish.

When using the flap disc on a weld

Flap discs are popularly used in making finishes on stainless and carbon steel. They are more preferable to the grinding wheel. This posits as a good choice because of its stable and extensive product life. It is much easier to control, provides superior comfort and generates low noise. The surface finish result is also incomparable.

A P40 coarse grit plus a flap disc would give your metal surface a plain and ready-to-paint look, especially the carbon steel. This is why the flap disc is used for more refined and quality finish.

The flap disc plus P80 grit would be a great tool to use for the first stage of the finishing. Less experienced welders should use P120 grit.

Conditioning and blending a welded joint

- The grinding process for the carbon steel is way easier when the metal is powder-coated.
- The stainless steel should be conditioned or blended further to achieve a number 4 or a highly refined finish.
- To blend out the initial scratch on carbon and stainless steel, use the medium grade Norton Vortex Rapid Blend
- To get a smear-free finish on the metal surface of stainless steel, use the Vortex disc in the 5000-6000 RPM range.
- In the case of scratched signs on the carbon steel, powder painting effectively masks the scratch.
- Refine the scratches on the carbon steel metal if the paint layer is very thin to not show up in the final layer.

At this point, the weld bead is gone, same with the welded seam. The metal surface is ready to be painted.

Time to Shine

Use the Norton Rapid Blend to blend out the surface imperfections. The number 4 finish is usually specified for projects like the balustrade or hand railings. This type of finish is a unique type of finish that can only be applied by specialists and most times, it is usually specified. It can be achieved with the belt or wheel.

To make the Number 4 finish, use a P120 abrasive belt and a medium-grade non-woven belt before making the final touch with the very fine woven belt. This will help you remove a little amount of the metal's surface without reducing its thickness. To achieve this, follow and maintain one direction when sanding.

When working on flat surfaces, use a satinex machine with wheels or belts with p80 coated flaps. Use it on a tube finishing machine alongside high-standard tubes and abrasive belts. Your metal is finished.

The number 4 finish is a technique that guarantees to give your metal a perfect shine.

A Short message from the Author:

Hey, I hope you are enjoying the book? I would love to hear your thoughts!

Many readers do not know how hard reviews are to come by and how much they help an author.

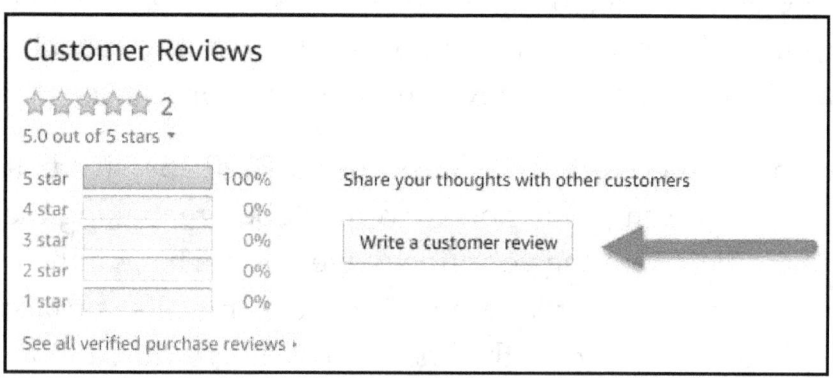

I would be incredibly grateful if you could take just 60 seconds to write a short review on Amazon, even if it is a few sentences!

>> Click here to leave a quick review

Thanks for the time taken to share your thoughts!

Chapter 5

Welding Techniques

There are five major techniques used in welding.

Some of them have been discussed partly under the type of welder sections.

Here, the techniques will be discussed individually and extensively.

MIG – Gas Metal Arc Welding (GMAW)

The MIG welding is a short term used to abbreviate the full term Metal Inert Gas Welding. This process was one of the earliest and was developed in early 1940. When it was initially developed, the name given to it was Gas Metal Arc. The MIG welding technique is usually considered semi-automated because the welder partly requires his skill. The machine is very smart or technically automated. The machine fills up the joints of the base metals continuously, so the welder doesn't need to change electrodes in between welds. The machine does most of the work, while the welder directs and monitors the process to watch out excesses and make little inputs where necessary. This is why this technique is considered the most favorable for first-timers or beginner welders.

This welding machine has four main parts that are important to be paid attention to in the welding process. They are listed for easy comprehension below;

- MIG welding power supply for providing electricity to create heat
- Wire feed system that feeds the wire to the weld joint from a spoon
- A handle that triggers and controls the wire feeder that feeds the wire to the weld joint from a spoon. This is very similar to a bicycle brake cable
- A shielding gas protecting the weld from air contaminants

MIG welding is mainly used in welding shops where the production level is very high and there is little possibility of wind blowing your shielding gas away. The main application areas of MIG welding are in the automotive and home improvement industry, manufacturing, and sheet metal work.

To work effectively, the MIG welding work requires three things;

- Electricity for heat production
- An electrode for filling joints
- Shielding gas for protecting the weld from air

The electrode is one very important thing in the welding process. The MIG welding requires a very small electrode that is automatically fed into the operator, which controls the amount of weld done per time.

The way manual welding works is that the welder squeezes the trigger of the MIG gun so that the electricity charges the electrode, and the feeder starts feeding the wire until the shielding gas is thoroughly feed through the gun nozzle.

As soon as the electrode contacts the metal, the arc starts to melt the weld joint and the filler metal just simultaneously while it is being shielded from air contamination by the shielding gas.

Advantages of the MIG welding process

1. This process is very easy and relatable for beginners.
2. It allows the welder to
3. It doesn't waste the weld materials.

4. There are no splatters or slags.

Disadvantages of the MIG welding process

1. Unlike other techniques, mistakes made in setting up the MIG welder is usually uncorrectable.
2. The machine is usually expensive, and second-hand machines aren't always the best choice
3. When this machine breaks down, it is usually very difficult to fix it up.

Setting up your MIG equipment

MIG uses a power supply that provides steady voltage, most notably, the Direct Current Electrode Positive (DCEP). Transformers and rectifiers are used in modulating the voltage from the power supply, thereby stabilizing and providing a good arc start and circuitry that prevents overloading. The material to be welded is connected to the power supply through a clamp to complete the circuit. A spool of wire is mostly housed in the power supply case coupled with a mechanism that feeds the wire via the cable toward the gun.

The MIG machine's "business end" is the hand-held gun. This gun comes with a trigger that simultaneously controls several functions. When the trigger is pulled, the welding wire becomes electrically charged and begins the motor drive, which automatically feeds the wire as you weld. The MIG welding has to be shielded from the atmosphere, mostly achieved when a shielding gas is directed over the weld area — and the trigger on the gun also controls the flow of gas. For some applications in MIG welding, a flux-cored wire is used either with a gas shield or alone.

Several MIG welding is achieved using a gas shield; mixes of carbon dioxide and argon/CO2 are very common. There is often a regulator or flowmeter in the gas bottle that helps to set the flow of gas. For light-duty welding, a good rule of thumb requires that you use around 20 cubic feet/ hour of gas flow. You can optimize the amount of gas used when you become skilled with the gun.

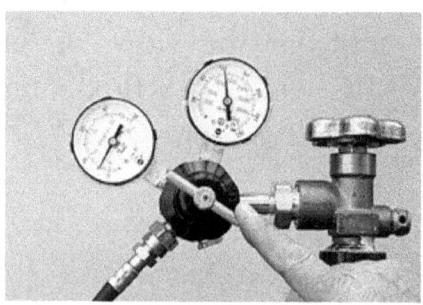

There are two important setups to be made on the welder before you begin the welding process; the voltage and the speed of the wire feed. Most MIG welder comes with a chart (like the one below), usually inside the hinged access cover that gives the suggested settings. However, these settings are per the type of material and thickness and the filler wire's diameter. These values should be used in adjusting the settings on the machine's face.

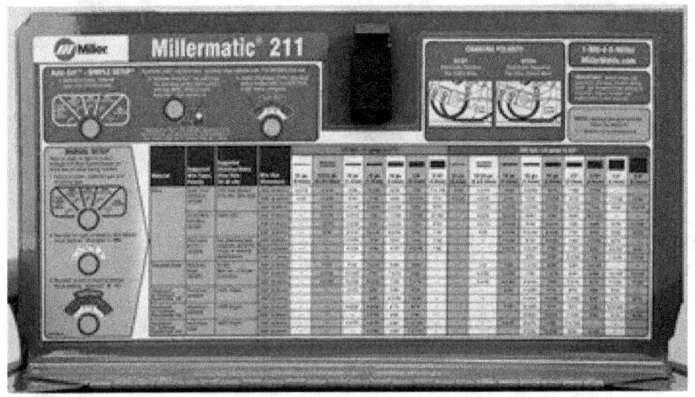

The Advanced Auto-Set™ technology pioneered by Miller helps you set the process, the wire diameter, and the material thickness; the machine will then automatically adjust the settings without a need to read the chart in many years to come.

In general, you should refer to your device's manual for a comprehensive installation process.

TIG – Gas Tungsten Arc Welding (GTAW)

This technique involves joining a range of metallic equipment like nickel, copper, alloys, titanium, and aluminum. The TIG technique is majorly used for high-quality welding. When you weld the sheet using a filler rod, this will give you a feel of how the puddle moves. In this technique, the tungsten is placed 2mm from the steel. There is a short flow of gas at this point, and the arc starts to use High frequency. The torch is kept in a stationary position for a short time so that the weld can form well. The filler rod is kept low so that the arc will ball it back. The arc length is long enough for the melting of the filler wire, and it melts backward so that it gets to reach the puddle.

Towards the end of the welding process, the torch is put off and brought back. Then the torch is held in a position that the flowing gas stops so that the tungsten and the weld pool are protected.

There are so many activities happening simultaneously, so it might not really go well, as you would need to focus your attention on several things all at once. Some things might go right, and others might go astray. Just place your first focus on getting the arc gap correctly, as it will set in tune the who welding process.

Make your practice natural, after which you can maintain your attention in the direction of the weld pool and the process of adding the filler metal. When these things are set in place, you will become capable of making neat welds with the TIG. Some major applications of this technique are in the aerospace, automotive, and aircraft construction industry and the repairs of auto bodies.

Advantages of TIG welding

1. It provides a tool that gives very detailed precision and it ensures less spattering.
2. With this technique, you can weld with various applications and different positions.
3. The TIG welding technique does complex metal welding on an extreme level
4. Unlike other tools that tend to consume its electrodes, the TIG uses non-consumable electrodes

Disadvantages of TIG welding

1. The TIG welding technique is a great time-consuming process
2. It can only be used by professionals, and it requires highly complicated appliances
3. The TIG welder makes use of inert gas, which is very costly.

Setting up your TIG equipment

Please refer to your device's manual for a complete and safe installation process. The diagram and instructions below are typical of a TIG welding system.

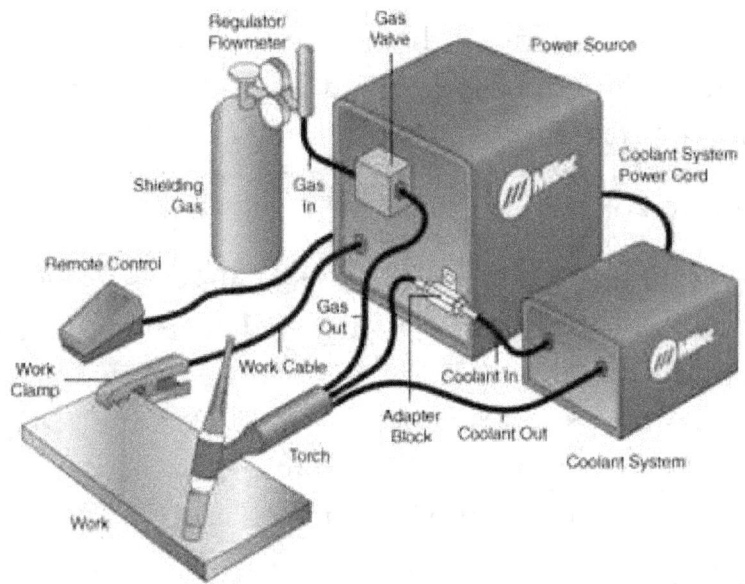

Connecting The Torch

When using an, use and plug the torch into your machine's front when using an air-cooled torch – use the adapter located in your accessory's package for this purpose. Also, you should connect the regulator and your gas hose.

Connecting The Remote Control

Plug your machine with your fingertip or foot pedal control.

Connecting The Work Clamp

Plug your machine with the work clamp (also called ground clamp); the other end should be clamped to your work table.

Selecting Polarity

When welding using steel and steel alloy, the setting of your amperage should be switched to Direct Current Electrode Negative (DCEN)— but for stick welding, it should be Direct Current Electrode Positive (DCEP). Similarly, when using aluminum for welding, your amperage setting should be switched to AC.

Preparing Tungsten

Your tungsten should be grinded to a certain point. If you use aluminum to weld, a ball will begin to form on the tungsten. Repoint the tungsten if the ball's diameter becomes the same as your tungsten. Ensure the point is about 2-1/2 times longer as the diameter while grinding in the long direction. Use a fine grinding wheel or a 200 grit for this purpose.

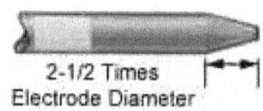
2-1/2 Times Electrode Diameter

The grinding wheel should not be used for other jobs else it will contaminate the tungsten resulting in lower weld quality.

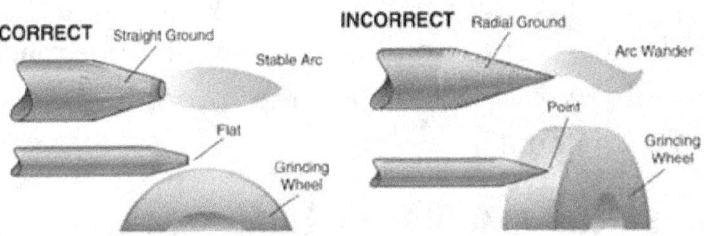

Assembleing The Torch

The back cap should be loosened, and the 3/32" diameter tungsten should be removed from your torch. Likewise, the nozzle should be removed, and also remove from your torch, the copper collet pieces. Put back the collet into your torch as well as the collet body and tighten. The nozzle should then be put back onto the torch.

Installing The Tungsten

The tungsten should be placed into the collet, then about 1/8 to ¼" should be left sticking out of the collet (shouldn't be more than the cap's diameter). Fasten the back cap.

Checking and Connecting The Power

Ensure the power supply being connected to is the same as your machine's rating (rating label can be found on the machine's unit). If a plug comes with your machine, connect it to the right power outlet when you are ready to weld. However, if no plug comes with your machine, it should be connected per the procedure in your machine's manual.

Stick – Shielded Metal Arc Welding (SMAW)

This welding technique is referred to as the type of welding that employs electrodes, also addressed as a stick. It can be used for welding all forms of ferrous metal and other types of metals. During this technique, the electrode carries the current and provides the metal weld. Immediately the high heat energy melts the rod and metal base to create the weld. Stick welding technique is majorly used in construction, the building of heavy equipment, repairs, and pipeline welding.

Strike the arc when starting the operation, the electrode is brought in contact with the workpiece. Light a match and slightly pull the metal away. The electrode pulls away from the base metal and causes the metal to twist if it sticks to the electrode.

Lift the electrode slightly and place it down on the base metal. The flux covers disintegrate as the electrode melts. Then a vapor is created that protects the weld from oxygen. The flux eventually provides a molten slag that covers the filler wire during the process that moves from the electrode. Just then, the slag starts to float to the surface and it protects the weld from environmental contaminants as it solidifies.

Advantages

1. It is effective to use in outdoor situations; in the rainy or windy season
2. The equipment is affordable when compared to others
3. This weld is a less comparable set.
4. It is very easy to change rods for different materials.

Disadvantage

1. It is a much more complicated process and requires speed.
2. It is time-consuming
3. This can provide excessive spatter
4. Welding rods can be replaced most consistently

Flux Corded Arc Welding (FCAW)

This technique involves the use of a tubular wire filled with flux. This flux tends to melt in the welding process, and it shields the weld pool from contaminating the atmosphere. It contains the core of the tubular electrode. FCAW is widely used in the mechanical and construction industries.

There are two basic processes of flux welding.

The first is self-shielded FCAW without shielding gas, and the second is gas shielded FCAW with shielding gas. The first type of FCAW is used outdoors as it is strong enough to withstand the wind from blowing it away.

The second type of FCAW allows the weld pool to be deoxidized and to some extent than the shielded FCAW, it allows for secondary shielding from the atmosphere.

FCAW evolved from the MIG welding process and it improves arc action, weld metal properties, weld appearance and metal transfer. The heat used for welding is produced by an arc that is situated in between a tubular electrode wire and the workpiece.

Equipment used in flux corded arc welding

1. A power source
2. Controls
3. Wire feeder
4. Welding gun
5. Welding cables

Advantages

1. It is highly productive and efficient
2. It guarantees good welding quality
3. This welding technique is simple and basic to use
4. It provides a very range of applications
5. The welding current is similar to other welding techniques; however, it tends to save deposited metal by 40%.
6. The flux welding technique involves high efficiency and deep penetration. All of this reduces the welding time and conserves the energy that would have been spent in the process of welding. Lesser gases are used in this case.
7. It is more efficient and saves more cost when compared with other techniques. It offers more quality and helps you produce more quantity at little cost.

Disadvantages

1. The flux wire produces a lot of smoke and fume.
2. Wire feeding, in this case, is difficult
3. After the flux wire is seamed, it cannot be saved or stored for long anymore.

Oxyacetylene Welding

This is the fusion of the welding equipment that uses heat for welding and adds it up with oxygen combustion and fuel gas like acetylene. A gas flame is then produced to melt the edges of the welded parts out. The molten metal is usually allowed to get solid together and a continuous joint is obtained. It is most suitable for joining 2 – 50mm thick metal sheets, which are usually used in addition to a filler metal of 15mm thickness. Oxyacetylene gas flame has a temperature of 3200 degrees C and can melt all types of commercial metals. Some popular applications of this type of welding technique are in sheet metal fabrication, joining of thin metals, and in the automotive and aircraft industries.

Equipment used in this technique

1. Oxygen and acetylene gas cylinders: These are the cylinder containing gases and oxygen. The

gland nut on the cylinder valve should be sealed and tightened to perfection.
2. Pressure regulators: this could also be referred to as a precision instrument. This regulator is responsible for controlling the flow of gases and pressure. This regulator should be used with only the gas that it has been prepared for, and it should be changed immediately there is damage.
3. Hoses: These are pipes through which gas is transported to the torch
4. Flame arrestors: This refers to a flashback arrestor fitted into the middle of the regulators and the hoses as a safety measure. They are used to prevent the flames from reaching the gas cylinders.
5. Welding torches: When the gases' pressure has been regulated, it is fed through respective hoses. Each gas is controlled with the valve that is present on the torch.
6. Economizers: This is a tool in the welder that saves acetylene and oxygen from wasting when the welding torch is no longer in use. It extinguishes automatically after the welding torch starts to rest.

The light-up procedure

The valves of oxygen are opened with the cylinder keys. They are usually opened by turning the cylinder valve spindle once. After which, the fuel gas control valve is opened and the regulator is adjusted to achieve the right pressure for working.

Then the gas is lit up using a spark lighter held at a right angle to the nozzle. Adjust the supply of the acetylene gas to the blowpipe when the flame begins to smoke. The oxygen level can be increased through the control valve.

The welding torch transports gases from the gas cylinders through the hoses. The nozzle at the back end of the torch systematically starts to emit flame. The flames are used to melt the edges of metals together. Set the oxygen level at 40 psi before the process begins, and the acetylene will be set at 10psi.

In cases where there will need to be an addition of filler metal, this would involve laying a hard deposit layer on the surface. To make this deposit, a flame containing excess acetylene gas is used. The base metal is usually heated until it starts sweating. As the rod melts into this surface in small deposits, the entire surface starts to build up.

This welding technique requires thorough practice; its high temperature can melt any type of commercial metal.

Advantages

1. It has the most portable and versatile process
2. It guarantees better control of the filler metal deposition rate
3. It is suitable for welding dissimilar metals
4. This gas welding provides better control over temperature
5. It requires low cost and easy maintenance

Disadvantages

1. It cannot be used for heavy sections
2. The oxyacetylene gas provides a low working temperature of gas flame
3. It involves a slow heating rate
4. The gas is unsuitable for reactive metals
5. A larger area is usually affected by heat than others
6. The shielding gas isn't so effective

7. The storage can be problematic and handling gases isn't always easy

Chapter 6

Welding Projects Ideas

There are so many projects you can try out as a beginner in welding. You just need to get the basic tools discussed in the previous chapters and you are good to go.

These projects are quite easy and very basic to make.

Classic Horseshoe Puzzle

The horseshoe puzzle is a classic that has been around for several years. If you have an animal reserve near you, this is a good project to try out for them. You can gift it to them or purchase a horse and make one for your horse. This chain joins two horses together permanently with a ring that looks irremovable, but it isn't permanent in itself. Also, I am so excited that this is our first project because it is very basic. Once you get the techniques used in this project, you won't have a problem understanding the ones to come. So, let's get into it already.

Supplies

- Two real horseshoes
- A metal ring with 1/5" thickness and 2.5" inside diameter.
- A 1.5" long and 1/8" thick chain
- Metal band saw

Procedures

Step 1: Use the saw to cut off the tips; this will give you a steel ready to be welded.

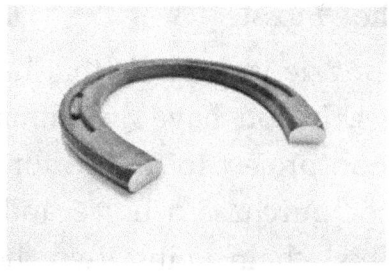

Step 2: Grind the tips of this metal using an angle grinder to make it clean and bare for welding. Before you do this, you have to hold the horseshoes to a sawhorse using a C-clamp. Position these shoes on your metal welding table that is put into position alongside some sample chips, very close to the chain.

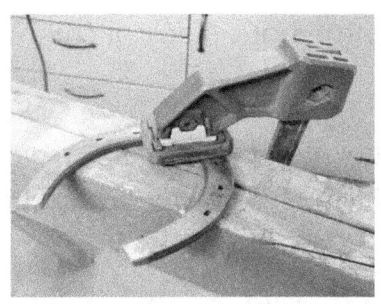

Step 3: Tack the chains to the horseshoe in a particular place. Create full weld beads on the edge to make the chain links stay firmly. Create a permanent open gap of 5/8" inch in between the two tips of the chain. You will get a very tight puzzle. It doesn't require any particular positioning to get it precisely joined together

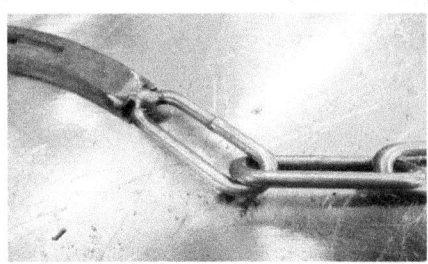

Step 4: Clean up the both sides of this weld with a steel brush.

Step 5: Insert the metal ring before welding the other side together with the weld. Clean up with a grinder.

Welded Steel Planters

This is a decorative piece that can be placed just anywhere in the house or an office. You can make any size of this and either place it on the table or the floor. This project doesn't cost too much. In two hours, you can build this decorative vase.

Supplies

- 14 gauge mild steel
- Plasma cutter

- Framing square
- MIG welder
- 4-1/2" grinder with a sanding disc
- PPE (leather gloves, welding helmet, safety glasses, jeans and long sleeves)

Procedures

Step 1: Use the plasma cutter and the framing square as a straight edge to make the following cuts on the steel;

- 4 pieces: 4-3/8" x 18" (sides)
- 4 pieces: 5-3/8" x 18" (front & back)
- 2 pieces: 4-3/8" x 5-3/8" (bottom)

Step 2: Use the 4-1/2" grinder and a sanding disc to clean up the sharp edges from the cutting process.

Step 3: Use a pair of right-angle magnetic clamps and welding tables to support the four sides of the planters first. After then weld the bottom caps to the planters. The end result is a perfect square bottom at each end. To ensure you get a perfect square, you can apply a few tack welds to hold the pieces while you check for a square. It will also help you to resist any form of deformation or unsettlement in case heat is directly applied to an area for too long.

You can also use an angle grinder to shine the weld joints and edges.

Step 4: You can put in your flowers and position your vase.

Floating Chain Wine Bottle Holder

This bottle holder is very easy to make, and it doesn't cost so much time and money. So, you can save some extra cash and make this solid wine holder yourself.

Supplies

- MIG welder
- A welding mask, gloves and appropriate clothing
- About 3.5 feet of steel chain
- Spray paint and clear coat
- An empty wine bottle

Procedures

Step 1: Use a jar lid as guide to make a circle of about 17.5" of chain. That is 14 links. Weld all the links together.

Step 2: Drape the chain over a container that can allow for a good length of draping. An empty paint can is a good option to consider. The chain should be positioned at around an 85-degree angle.

Weld the vertical chain together without disrupting the bottom link.

Step 3: After the weld, take away the paint container and make a circle 1 3/8" to 1 1/2" diameter at the top of the "stem" or the draping. Weld the circle. Check the

size of the circle with an empty wine bottle. Then wrap the chain around the neck of the wine bottle and weld it all to the dangling end.

Step 4: Clean up the metal and apply two coats of spray paint. The semi-gloss black is very attractive. Coat with two coats of clear coat.

Steel Prototype Fabrication

This staircase can be used on the porch or any area in the house that needs stairs. You don't need to pay an architect to craft this for you. This project will teach you how to fabricate the weld completely. It involves welding, cutting, drilling and tapping. You can make a larger staircase once you get the basis of this project. This is just a prototype.

Supplies

- 1" thick plywood for making the tread.
- 2" thick plywood for the handrails.
- 3/16" thick 1" square tube for railing
- 3/16" thick metal sheets for CNC parts.
- Nuts, bolts and washers.

Procedures

Step 1: 1" thick Plywood tread was designed digitally and cut by CNC routing. Make four drills at the corners using the bottom steel frame support.

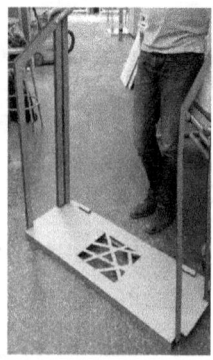

Step 2: Sand the plywood pieces to prepare them for welding.

Step 3: Use the 3/16" thick steel plate parts to get accuracy in joints.

Step 4: Use a horizontal band saw to cut 3/16" thick 1" square tube steel balusters to desired lengths.

Step 5: Use the MIG welder to weld the steel tubes into the waterjet cut steel plate that connects the floor. Frame

the steel tube in between the two opposite balustrades to establish a strong base for the tread.

Step 6: Use the metal grinder to grind the metal and cut down the excess weld.

Step 7: Paint the metal pieces to give them a smooth and perfect finish.

Step 8: Make different joints by welding, cutting and using nuts and bolts

Step 9: Get a Steel plate connector to connect the balustrade and the wooden handrail.

Step 10: This is how the staircase looks after the fabrication and painting.

Garden Vines Metal Trellis

If you have a garden in your yard, you should consider adding this metal trellis, it will give your garden a unique facelift. It serves as a shelf to place your vines and plant vases. Also, it will interest you to know that it is very easy to make

Procedures

Step 1: The very first step to Sketch It Up!

You might not need to make a new sketch up, except you want to make a different model using a different type of measurement. Sketching up makes it easy to create 3-D versions with accurate precision or picture of what is in your head.

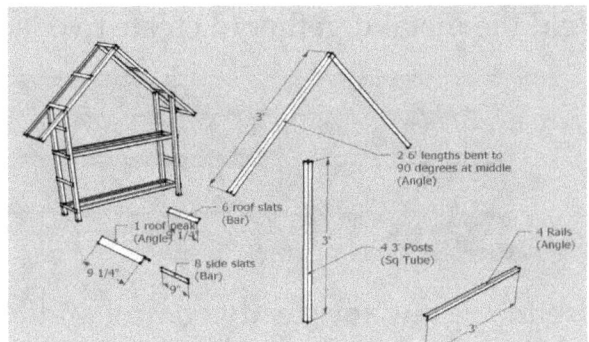

Step 2: Use the sketch above to make your cuts. You can also make your cuts from your own measurements.

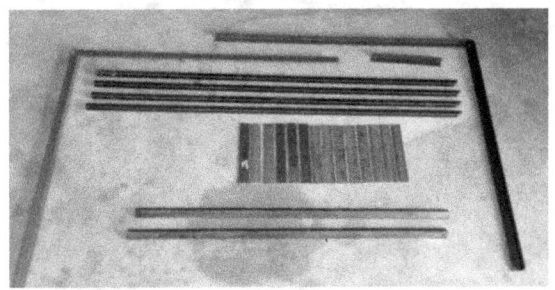

Step 3: To create jigs, lay out the wood and clamp them side by side. Also, sand the metal at this point.

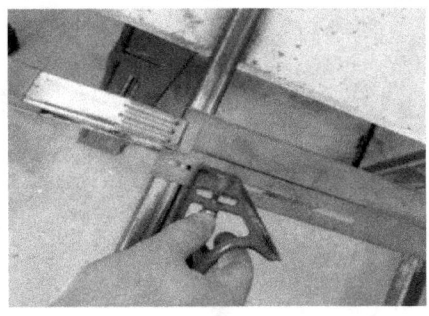

Step 4: Weld the metal together to create two ladders

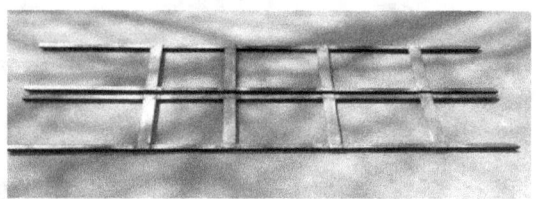

Step 5: Use the jigsaw for steady control and clamp the steel just behind the bend point. Pulling the arms to 90-degrees was very easy. Then paint and coat the metal.

Step 7: Mount it on a smooth plane ground, your trellis is ready.

Mini Atomium

Atomium can be used for illustration in schools or just as a decoration piece. It is quite technical, but you can creatively follow the process.

Supplies

- 9x stainless steel ball bearings with a 40 mm diameter
- 12x stainless steel 70.8 mm rod of 8mm diameter
- 8x stainless steel 56.4 mm rod of 8mm diameter
- A small stainless steel 20mm rod of 8mm diameter
- A metal plate of 360 mm by 205 mm and a minimum of 5 mm in depth

- A piece of wood of 40 mm by 48 mm by 20 mm
- A piece of nice wood of 235 mm by 100 mm by 45 mm
- TIG welding machine
- Welding clamp + safety gear
- A drill
- A milling machine
- Ruler

Procedures

Step 1: Organize your plans

Analyze the structure of the Atomium. As it seems, it appears to be a cube sitting on one edge of the floor. There is a sphere at the corner of every cube, and the cube has one sphere that links it to the other 8 balls on the corner of the cube.

You might face a challenge in trying to position the center sphere at the center of the cube. One easier way to do it is to place dimensions face made by 4 opposite spheres of the cube plus the center sphere. What you eventually have is a rectangle that is made of 4 spheres.

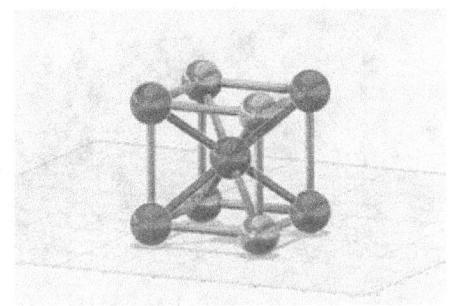

Step 2: Build a welding jig that will hold the ball bearing in place while you weld the 8mm rods that links them together. To achieve that, take a steel plate and drill holes for the balls to sit; you will weld the balls to the sticks. Drill another 2 holes that will be some distance apart and form a square for the sides. Drill holes of 15mm. The hole located in the middle of the rectangle has been placed at the intersection of the 2 diagonals of the rectangle.

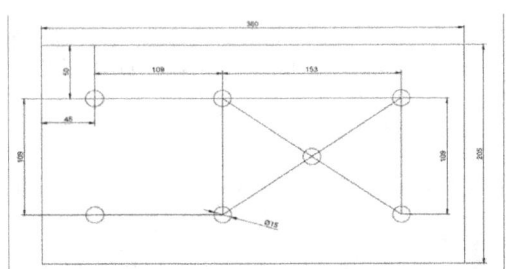

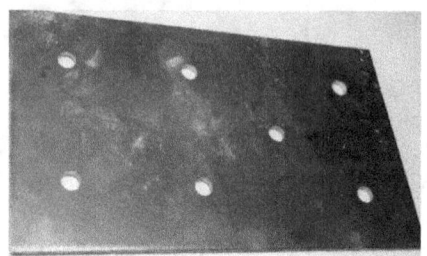

Step 3: Use a piece of wood like the one in the picture to retain the stick and ball in a slot while you weld. Use the first piece of wood of 40 mm. On the 40x48mm face, mill a 8mm wide, 5mm deep slot in the long middle of the face.

Step 4: Weld It. Align the stick to the sphere and weld for long.

Tip: Try not to weld for too long as the wood will go on fire.

Step 5: Make it nice. Build a small stand to hold it in place, and weld a little piece of stick to hold into the sculpture and place it inside the wood of 235mm with a drilled hole. Sand the edges and apply coating to make your Atomium as beautiful as this.

Steel Rose

This is a highly creative project; although steel roses are not so common, you can make one for decoration sake and see how people would react to it

Supplies

- Stainless steel pipe
- Mig welder
- Plasma cutter

Procedures

Step 1: Get your pieces of Stainless-Steel Pipe

Step 2: Draw spherical drop shapes on the metal, as many spheres as you wish and cut out the pieces.

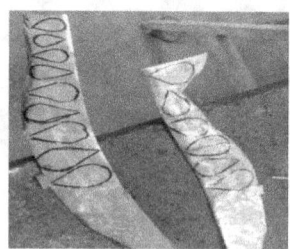

Step 3: Take the pieces and start bending them into a flower shape.

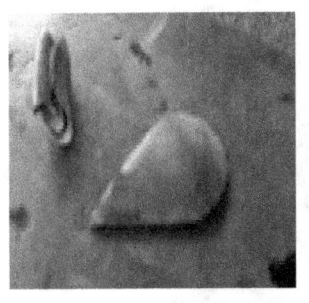 

Step 4: Weld the rose once you have joined all of them together to form an attractive flower.

Step 5: Cut more pieces to make petals for the flower.

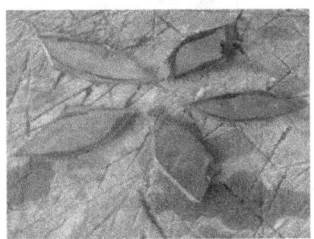

Step 7: Make this branch with one single flower.

Step 8: Join rose to the petals and then to the branch.

Bar Stool

This is a simple bar stool that can be made by using angle iron.

Procedures

Step 1: Make a focus to the height of 1 ½ inches.

Step 2: The form's base was made using pieces of framing lumber that was 3 1/2" wide. These pieces needed a bevel cut so they would angle upward to the top of the form tube.

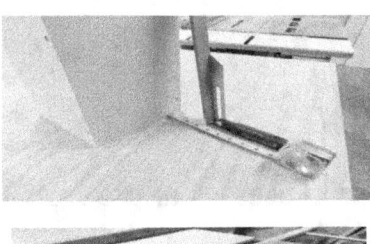

Step 3: The beveled base pieces are usually fixed together, alongside the nail, with scrap pieces of plywood that were glued and nailed in place.

Step 4: With this form, you can't make mistakes on leg location and length. Just lower each leg and cut first. The insides of this form were marked using a paint pen.

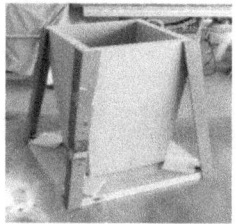

Step 5: Weld four pieces of angle iron to make the top metal. These was marked using a framing square and paint pen, and it was cut using a bandsaw.

Step 7: Weld pieces of iron to make the footrest of the leg frame for this stool.

Step 8: Weld all the lower parts of this stool together.

Step 9: For the top wood, you can use any available hardwood of your choice. In this project, the wood used is from a walnut tree and was measured at 2 1/4" thick boards.

Route the edges with a round-over bit and sand the surfaces with sandpaper of 100 to 220 grit.

Step 10: Spray the legs and add finishing to the wood.

Step 11: Screw in the wooden seat from the bottom of the metal seat.

Steel and Coffee Sack Footstool

Imagine you see this in a furniture store with a price tag of a few dollars. Would you believe you can make this yourself without much cost and stress? This footstool is very comfortable to use.

Supplies

- 40mm Box Section Steel

- 18mm Plywood
- 3/4" Plywood
- 2" Upholstery Foam
- Metal Cutting Saw
- Angle Grinder
- 40 Grit Flap Disc
- Black Spray Paint
- Spray Adhesive
- Chalk Paint Pen
- Upholstery Tacks
- Coffee Sack

Procedures

Step 1: Cut the 40 mm steel using your Mitre Saw. Cut it into 2 x rectangles to start, one for the top and one for the bottom. Cut this footstool with the measurement; 40cm x 50cm.

Step 2: You can use any welder of your choice to weld this frame together. Next, use a welding hammer to chip off the slag that forms over the welds. Grind this metal with a 40-grit flap disc on my angle grinder.

Step 3: Cut down 4 bits of steel at 25cm each for the vertices. Make three legs for the steel. It is more stable than it looks; you don't necessarily need a fourth leg.

Step 4: Make tabs to hold the wood and foam base onto the frame. Measure up to 4 x 6cm long strips of scrap steel. Swap out the flap disc for a metal cutting disc. Mark a center hole to drill; the hole should be located a little distance from the frame and closer to the middle of the footstool. Drill a 4mm hole in each of the tabs.

Step 5: Spray the frame with a shiny paint and allow for 2-3 hours to dry.

Step 6: Mark the exact size of 18mm plywood. Use the wood to mark out and cut out the size for the foam. The foam used here is the 2" thick upholstery foam. Spray adhesive on the wood and the foam. Allow it 2-3 mins to get perfectly stuck together.

Step 7: Before adding the coffee bag, use some thick wadding in between. Trim it down a little and use a staple gun to pin it down.

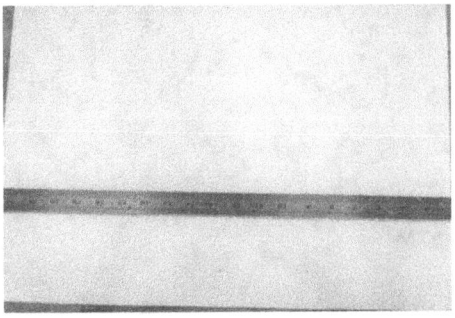

Step 8: Get a simple coffee bag and trim it down to size, you can fold it several times if the bag happens to be too long.

Step 9: Use black upholstery tacks to hammer through the sack, wadding and straight into the plywood. Make an even distance between every tack. Then screw the top to the frame.

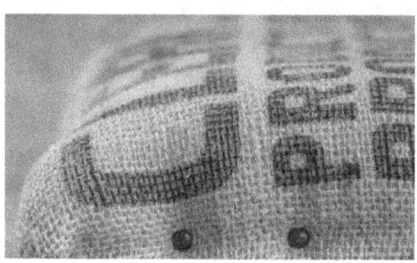 

Metal Base Outdoor Table

This outdoor table is one of the most attractive there is, and it is very easy to make with just basic tools.

Supplies

- Router
- Grinder
- Cutoff Saw
- 3/4" Steel Bar
- 2 1/2" Steel Flat Bar
- 3/4" Steel Angle Iron
- Tropical Hardwood Decking Boards

- Matte Black Paint

Procedures

Step 1: Layout and Cut the Legs using the 3/4'" bar stock.

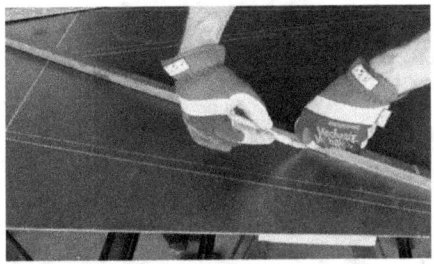

Step 2: Grind the angles on the ends and tack the pieces together, after which you can weld each area. Use a 7" grinder to smoothen everything down.

Step 3: Cut some 2-1/2" flat bar to size such that it can be welded as an attachment to the table. Add some holes along the flat bar. This will allow you to attach every of

the board with screws. Weld the table legs to the flat bar with a full bead for a strong joint.

Step 5: Connect the table legs with long stretcher for stability. Lay out the left over bar, mark it and weld it in place.

Step 6: Cut down the pallet using a table saw to 2-1/2" wide each. Use a 45-degree chamfer bit to cut the boards and reduce its thickness to ¾" to make them have the shape of table legs

Step 7: Use the cold saw to cut down miters on the metal. Weld these metals together on individual corners to prevent warping of the frame.

Step 8: Apply finish to the metal and coat to the wood.

Step 9: Assemble the Table using 5/8" screws.

Chapter 7

Resolving Common Welding Mistakes

There are many common mistakes in welding that some amateurs struggle with.

Several welders worry about providing welding quality assurance that they tend to make very common mistakes that they could have ordinarily avoided. Wanting to give quality isn't a bad thing, but when you get so engrossed in the pursuit of quality, it could cause you to have an oversight of the basics.

Welding requires a lot of focus, as there are so many details that need to be carried out. You need to focus on equipment usage, filler metals, consumables, and techniques. With this focus and a little know-how, you can avoid these mistakes.

Here is a list of mistakes:

- Repurposing old equipment:

Old equipment is usually very affordable and available, so many welders use this in place of getting a new one. As good as this might be, these equipment can cause extra repair costs and maintenance. The welder doesn't know this at the point of purchase; it is a problem that is usually discovered much more later. Using old or dilapidated power sources, welder, generators, wire feeders and other technical tools is a NO. Indeed, new tools and equipment can be pretty costly, but they save you the stress of troubleshooting and repairs.

Also, new equipment works faster and grants you a quick return on investment (ROI) and greater long-term savings by offering you

- o Reduced weld prep time
- o Unified controls that simplify user operation and training
- o Low amperage draw that reduces operating costs.
- o Higher wire feed speeds for welding

To confirm this, you can perform a very thorough cost-saving analysis before purchasing a new equipment.

- Overlooking training opportunities

If you want to have a headway in your career, you have to invest time and money in training, you have to go for workshops and watch video trainings. They will expound your mind bigger and educate you on what you need to know. Proper training can give you a competitive edge over others with less-skilled labor. If you want to make an outstanding career in welding, you would have to enroll in some technical college.

- Disregarding MIG gun consumables

When a person consistently overlooks the importance of consumables, it could lead to a host of problems like:

- Poor shielding gas coverage
- Weld defects
- Unscheduled downtime for changeover
- Premature contact – tip failure

Avoid the temptation to purchase less expensive consumables, you will be purchasing low-quality materials that won't satisfy you before they become useless and they could be highly consequential.

Always go for the appropriate style of nozzle and properly trim liners according to the manufacturer's recommendation.

- Ignoring preventive maintenance

This is not only wrong but hazardous. However, it is the most overlooked practice and the commonest mistake. It helps to keep mistakes downtime, and it is critical to reducing unscheduled downtime and keeping the costs low. Preventive measures include regular inspection and care of the power source, welding gun, consumables, and operating system. Other detailed preventive maintenance practices are:

- o Tightening loose connections
- o Monitor a liner and track the length of time it stays before it gets bad
- o Scan for consumables, and replace any tool if needed
- o Constantly inspect the gun and the consumables to be sure they contribute to the quality of the weld.
- Improper weld preparation

The welding process involves many stages and processes. These processes and stages must be mastered to a large extent before the welder starts welding; this is why this book extensively discusses what you must know as a welder. Skipping any stage is usually very consequential. One basic stage not to joke with is the preparation stage. Skipping this stage can lead to reworking, work defects, and scrapped parts. Here's a short list of the basic preparation that needs to be done before you start building a weld.

- Clean the base material to prevent contaminants like dirt from entering the weld pool.
- Follow the weld parameter settings highlighted in the welding procedure specification.
- Be careful not to use too much anti-spatter as it enters the weld joint and causes irreversible problems or damages the nozzle's insulator.
- Properly tack all the parts together to avoid extra anti-spatter and poor weld preparation
- Do a double-check for bad or damaged cable connections which can result in a drop in voltage level.

- Improper filler metal storage and handling

Sometimes, even after you get a quality filler metal piece, the area of storage could also affect the metal and cause it to have multiple faults. You should store your metal in a very dry and contaminant-free space with a relatively constant temperature until it is ready for use. You could also refer to the manufacturer's recommended storage practices.

- Shielding gas inconsistencies

Shielding gas comes in different sizes and mixtures. Ensure to use the correct gas type to reduce spatters, post-weld clean up, and prevent defects.

When using other non-carbon steel metals, it is required that the gas selection method is changed because it is not the same. The gas mixes at 5% for stainless steel. For aluminum, the gas should be 100%. These wire specifications are usually written on the wire specification's sheet.

- Improper preheat or interposes temperature control

Some people even totally skip this procedure. Hence, they expose their metal to cracking because preheating is essential in reducing the metal's cooling rate after the welding process. The type of material determines the level of preheating temperature. Some WPS or welding codes come with these details.

Specifically, when welding carbon steel, ensure that the heated area is approximately 3 inches on the sides of the weld joint. Start welding when the metal is at preheat temperature for the best result.

- Purchasing filler metals based on cost

I have already stated that being too cost conscious in your welding practice can cost you unbargained stress. Due to the drive for cost savings, you might get low-quality filler metal for a very cheap and affordable price. This can reduce your productivity level and result in other issues like:

- o Weld defects
- o Excessive splatter
- o Poor wire feeding

Using a poor filler metal is highly consequential and will demand that you apply anti-spatter, post-weld grinding and rework. It would also require extra work and result in excess release of energy when it could have been solved using a higher quality filler metal. Say no to cheap materials!

- Using the wrong MIG gun size

Your MIG gun size has to be accurate; using a high or low amperage of MIG gun can tamper with the rate of your productivity and your machine's efficiency. A MIG gun of low size in particular, helps to reduce excessive costs and fatigue. It also allows you to gain flexibility. MIG with higher amperage will require higher efforts to control, more periods of welding, and a higher amperage gun to discourage overheating.

Asides from this, eight other forms of mistakes could happen in the process, and sometimes these things happen due to ignorance.

- Spatter

You might have come across this term several times in this work and wonder what a spatter is; you might have probably checked your dictionary. This is a simple word used to describe drops of molten material around the welding arc, produced from high current in welding, poor gas shielding, incorrect polarity. To prevent spatters, the welding current should be moderately high and placed under close watch. The welder should check the consumable polarity and the type of shielding gas; this all helps to control the spatter, reduce or prevent it totally.

- Porosity

Another very sad defect that could be caused by neglect. This is directly caused by the absorption of hydrogen, nitrogen, and oxygen in the weld pool. Direct causes of porosity are excessive moisture, grease, paint, poor gas shielding, and rust. To avoid this porosity, the welder should place the metal on the welder to re-bake it. Fresh welding consumables could also be used. Conduct checks in the welding torch for leakage. Clean plate edges can help to prevent it too. Finally, run checks on the type of shielding gas, the nozzle of the gas, and the welding torch.

- Slag inclusions

This refers to small and tiny flux particles that get trapped in the weld metal that prevents the full weld penetration. The only way to avoid this slag is to keep and maintain flux-coated consumables. Also, having a correct voltage, correct current, and good arc qualities is required to ensure that quality welds come with full fusions during the welding process.

- Undercut

This defect usually occurs when the voltage is excessively high. The arc is very long itself; it is possible to occur if the electrode happens to be inequivalently large compared to the plate's thickness, the travel speed is too much, amongst other things. To control the occurrence, the welder should monitor the travel speed and ensure that it is moderate. It is also good to check and monitor the appliance and usage of the electrode available. The welder should avoid using an extremely large electrode, it could cause more molten metal, and when they become too big, it would create an undercut. Also, monitor the weave level, and don't allow the vertical plate to be near the electrode when doing the horizontal fillet weld.

- Cracks

In every sphere, cracks are major defects that could be highly consequential in itself. Small cracks could possess the potentials to become extremely large after a while. Some welders think the solution to every crack is adding a material to fill in space. The solution to cracks is to grind the cracks out and make new welds. This involves a lot of stress and could be prevented by spending quality time grinding, filing, cleaning, and sharpening the plates' edges to fit well.

- Incomplete penetration and fusion

This occurs when fusion fails to happen on one particular side of the weld and the joint root. It also occurs when both sides are not fused. This issue occurs in consumable electrode processes most often; at this time, the weld is automatically positioned as the electrode wire or rod is consumed in the arc. There are so many solutions that can be applied, solutions like electrodes diameter size almost equal to the root size, using wider root gap. You could also use low travel speed to do a weave in between the edges during welding.

- Deformation

This is like the opposite of cracks, cracks leave open holes, but this involves having excess weld beads. Some solution to this problem involves welding from both sides of the metal joint, disorientating the original sequence of weld, using a larger electrode, and making sufficient clamping. You could also deoptimize the risk of deformation by systematically orchestrating simple passes and changing the weld joint position.

- Incorrect wire delivery

Noises like chattering sounds under the cable of the gun could be a sign of a problem. It could be a pointer to the problem of a poor delivery system. The welder would have to ensure the right setup and maintenance of this equipment. While running an overall checking on the welding equipment system, ensure to do a round check on the size of wire to be used. Constantly monitor and check if it is obsolete and requires change. For the drive rolls, you should also check them constantly to ensure the drive rolls and guide tube are within close reach.

The end... almost!

Hey! We've made it to the final chapter of this book, and I hope you've enjoyed it so far.

If you have not done so yet, I would be incredibly thankful if you could take just a minute to leave a quick review on Amazon

Reviews are not easy to come by, and as an independent author with a little marketing budget, I rely on you, my readers, to leave a short review on Amazon.

Even if it is just a sentence or two!

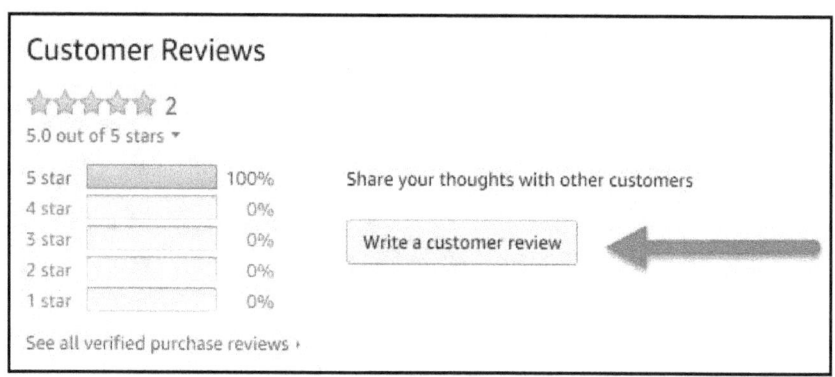

So if you really enjoyed this book, please...

\>> Click here to leave a brief review on Amazon.

I truly appreciate your effort to leave your review, as it truly makes a huge difference.

Chapter 8

Welding Frequently Asked Questions

1. What is the strongest welding technique?

The Tungsten Inert Gas (TIG), also known as GTAW welding technique, produces the cleanest and strongest welds. Through this technique, you can make real strong welds that are used in routine applications. One reason why all welds made with the TIG welder is usually much stronger is due to the TIG welding equipment's efficiency.

Several available uses for the TIG welders enable the welder to make strong welds in the aluminum material. They are mainly used to select and position root passes in square root groove joints. These groove joints are majorly used in fabricating metal cabinets, which makes the TIG welds a perfect option again because it provides good aesthetics.

Unlike other welds that seem attractive and weak in themselves, the TIG has a good aesthetic and it is also strong.

The huge disadvantage of TIG welding is that it takes more time to practice and master.

Other techniques like MIG welding are used to fabricating welds of varying strength in practical applications.

2. Is weld strength dependent on the ability of the weld to penetrate the bead plate?

The strength of a weld isn't just based on its possibility to penetrate the bead plate. This is far from the basic thing; the tensile and shear usually measure the weld's strength. All these welding types are categorized under arc welding. Arc welding involves fusing two separate pieces of base metal as one, so they become blended. This process is also called fusion.

There is no relationship between the strength of the weld and the weld bead. To ensure a great weld strength, the welder is to make use of the right filler metal. The filler metal is an electrode that is sharply in charge of adding and selecting chemical materials to make the weld bead up. It is also described as consumable electrodes.

3. How can I ensure that my filler metal yields the best result?

The welding position determines to a very large extent how the filler wire or metal will turn out. Some type of filler metals is purely fluid as they come in molten form. Hence if care is not taken and the weld isn't well-positioned, the metal can drip and cause harm to the welder, especially if it is positioned in a vertical or overhead position. Also, the position of the base metal in the process of welding determines the possibility of the weld bead penetrating all the way through the metal to the joint.

4. What type of metals can Oxyacetylene weld?

This technique is used in welding all commercial metals. It is most effective with low carbon and alloy steel, cast iron, and wrought iron.

5. What are the best shielding gases used in TIG welding?

The best shielding gas for welding is the Pure Argon. It can cope with all the common materials and metals. For specialized projects, the Helium and Argon Helium gases are mixed and used.

6. Can the oxyacetylene technique be used in welding aluminum?

Yes, this welding technique can be used for almost all types of steel.

7. Why is tensile strength important?

This concept has not been explained in this book, so I'm going to define tensile strength. This term is also called Ultimate Tensile Strength or Ultimate strength. It refers to the maximum degree of stress and pressure that a material can bear and sustain before breaking. Causes of strength might be stretching or pulling of the metal. Tensile strength can be measured in welding applications by pounds-force per square inch. Usually, when you purchase a new metal, you should find the product package's tensile strength. If you select a filler wire with low tensile strength, you are at the risk of making a weak weld.

8. How important is weld strength?

There is a specific weld strength requirement for every project. The amount or level of weld strength you need is dependent on the project you are making. However, strength is not the only thing to consider when talking about welds. The length, size, and spacing are also as important as the strength of the weld. So, don't focus all your attention on the weld's strength and ignore every other area.

9. What are the contents of the TIG welding set?

A regulator with a pressure gauge and a flow meter to monitor the flow of pressure and heat.

An argon cylinder, the size depends on the job requirement, as it comes in varying sizes.

A torch that consists of an argon gas hose, a welding lead, a ceramic nozzle, collet, and a tungsten rod for creating an arc.

A filler wire in place of the filler metal to act as an electrode

The transformer or rectifier

10. What is the soaking period for carbon steel material and alloy steel material during stress-relieving?

The soaking period for every metal is peculiar to it; for carbon steel, the soaking period used in stress-relieving is one hour. For alloy steel material, the soaking period is two hours.

11. What is the effect of the quantity of hydrogen-induced in the weld metal?

The hydrogen is usually excessive in the weld metal; this tends to make the material more brittle and susceptible to cracking. This crack is often called hydrogen-induced or delayed crack. To avoid this, you would have to allow the metal C for one exact hour in a mother oven C to 300 electrodes before it is backed down at 250 and then allowed to cool down.

12. What can be used to control the porosity in metal?

The measure of solid solubility in liquid or solid welded metals is the most essential criterion for stabilizing the weld's porosity. The gas reactions, in some sense, regulates porosity.

13. What is the Shielded Metal Arc Welding (SMAW) specifically used for in the welding procedure?

This welding type is majorly used in special industrial fabrication applications, and it is used in fabricating steel structures. It can also be used in the field or the shop.

14. What makes Gas metal arc welding different from Flux-cored arc welding?

The flux-cord technique is used specifically to make portable applications used in making thick welds and out-of-position metals. On the other hand, GMAW is the most common type of industrial welding machine, as it is faster than the others and has a continuous electrode feed. It is majorly used for fabricating metals in the field.

15. What are the most important skills for a welder to have?

Anyone interested in the craft of welding should be well knowledgeable in the theoretical aspects of welding. The person should also be part of an active learning process. Above all this, problem-solving skills and critical thinking skills are of utmost importance, as welding could be quite technical. It requires heads that can read beyond the surface to effectively and successfully manage the process.

16. How can I set up a MIG welder?

To set up a machine, you have to follow the instruction in the package of the instrument. This is because every brand producer or manufacturer specifies their own specification of the tool. However, in the MIG welder, there is a basic setup process; this process is very important and requires proper knowledge of the settings. With other welders, your wrong setup could easily be corrected, but every setup error with the MIG welder is highly consequential.

17. How can I perfect my welding skills?

One key strategy to perfecting your welding skill is to learn with all the welder types. You will learn how to manipulate techniques on different welders. Also, select a welding technique that allows you to be comfortable while you work?

18. How much should a MIG welder stick out?

The electrode should stick out about ¾ of an inch. Although a lesser length is still okay, the longer the wire stick, the more difficult it is for the shielding gas to do what it is supposed to do. The flow rate of the shielding gas also needs to be right for the stick-out. When the gas is too much, it could result in turbulence, and when the gas is too little, it can't supply enough shielding gas. Keep your stick-out length at ¾ to ¼ inches.

19. What is the best MIG welding technique pattern to use?

The steady motion pattern is the easiest and basic pattern used in MIG welding, as it requires the machine to be set properly. This is the method most robots use in welding, and it is quite straightforward. It also produces a perfect weld in just any position. The hotter the settings become, the easier and faster the process of welding.

www.ingramcontent.com/pod-product-compliance
Lightning Source LLC
Chambersburg PA
CBHW050319120526
44592CB00014B/1978